PHIL CHEALE

MY GOD CAN BE TRUSTED

AT HOME & ABROAD

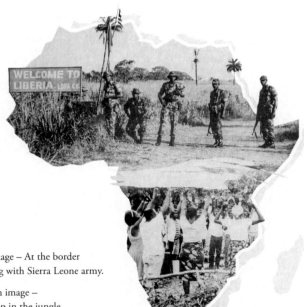

Top image – At the border
crossing with Sierra Leone army.

Bottom image –
Worship in the jungle.

Dedication

To the memory of my great friend
Richard Cole, promoted to glory 2006.

Published by

Maurice Wylie Media
Inspirational Christian Publisher

Acknowledgments

This story would never have been written without the encouragement and involvement of my many friends including Dr. Ruth Van Reken and Pastor Chris Justice, with a final push from Mariusz and Gosia Gogolin.

Thank you to my wife, Sylvia, who has endured and supported me with great loyalty in all the many places we have lived and worked. She has always been the homemaker, even though at times that home was sometimes in strange and unexpected places.

To my children Christine, Amanda, Beverley, and Richard, thank you also for your encouragement and support in recording these experiences. For you and our twelve grandchildren, and an increasing number of great grandchildren, this book is for you.

Foreword

As believers in Jesus Christ, our calling is to follow Him and pursue the destiny He planned for each of us. Many of us choose to go our own way, leaving God out of the equation of our lives. But for Phil Cheale and his wife Sylvia, they chose to follow the Lord, and this is the story of their extraordinary lives.

My husband and I have known Phil and Sylvia for more years than we can remember. We first met them on their return to the UK after working as missionaries in Sierra Leone and Liberia. Our first impression was of a couple who were quietly spoken and humble. As they endeavoured to 're-enter' our culture after living in Africa for many years, and settle their four children into local schools and a western way of life, we saw their trust in the God who provides all our needs.

This book is the story of their lives … often they faced extreme danger and found themselves in situations they would not have chosen to be in. However, as Phil describes so vividly and often humourously, God never once let them down and always kept them safe.

So, who is this book for? Having read it from cover to cover in one sitting – unable to put it down, I would recommend it to anybody who is considering being a missionary in another culture; to any new believer wondering what the Christian life is all about, or to anybody who is in a rut with their faith.

We may not all be called to be missionaries in warzones or in cultures that are alien to us. But as followers of Jesus, we are all called for something. As Phil writes, 'When our decision to follow God is underpinned by our complete trust in Him, we begin to realise that we can accomplish every task He asks and expects of us.'

Julia Fisher, Broadcaster, author and tour guide.

Contents

Introduction

"He is no fool who gives what he cannot keep to gain that which he cannot lose." —Jim Elliot

I need to get something straight right from the very start. If my story is not grounded firmly upon what I believe was God's will for my life, then I have been a fool, and my trust in God would have a shaky foundation. On the other hand, if every step of my remarkable journey was taken in obedience to the revealed will of God, trusting in Him, then all the resources of heaven's provision, protection, and peace were released upon me and my family, even during times of need and danger, as well as seasons of great blessing.

As the writer to the Hebrews wrote in Hebrews 11:6, *"It is impossible to please God without faith,"* and in verse 8, "It was faith that made Abraham obey when God called him . . . and Abraham *left his own country without knowing where he was going"* (emphasis added). Certainly, that final statement has been my experience. So many times, having left my own country, I encountered not only the unexpected but also several life-endangering moments. Yet it was my belief that God always had a purpose for me being in each of those situations, during which I received His divine protection and provision without which I very much doubt that I would have survived.

I do not regard myself as a particularly religious person. As far as I am concerned, I'm just a simple working man who encountered a life-changing experience with the living God. The result was that a wonderful relationship developed between God and me. This relationship was always a bit one-sided, for not only did God initiate it, He also sustained it. Amazingly to me, God transformed my life in such a way that I was blessed to be sent as a missionary to Africa where I made many friends. Because of these friendships, I made multiple visits to Sierra Leone and Liberia throughout the civil war years, to assist them with their own vision for their people.

Although I was considered a failure at school, seen by many as a weak Christian and a disappointment to my Christian parents, God in His grace and mercy called, equipped, and directed me in ways I can only describe as miraculous. My conversion to Christianity was radical; my acceptance to Bible college beyond explanation; my marriage vital to all that happened; my ministry beyond expectation; and the tasks assigned to me by God were extraordinary. Such life-changing encounters can only be explained, as Paul wrote, by the fact that there is a God in heaven who *"Chose the foolish things of the world to shame the wise; chose the weak things of the world to shame the strong, chose the lowly things of this world and the despised things—and the things that are not—to nullify the things that are, so that no one may boast before him"* 1 Corinthians 1:27-30 NIV. This God not only can but has done *"immeasurably more than all we ask or imagine, according to his power that is at work within us"* Ephesians 3:20-21 NIV.

Amazingly, these verses summarise the way I understand my relationship with God, for He placed me before prisoners and presidents, the rich and the poor, the wise and the foolish for the sole purpose of proclaiming His Word at the right time to the right people and often during times of their greatest need.

I recognise that it was God who has orchestrated every event in my life, from the first day that I was "born again" by the power of the Holy Spirit, to this current time. God, through the inspiration and revelation of the Holy Spirit, led me to a Bible college for training, then, through a period of isolation, into the Sahara Desert where I learnt to listen to Him speaking to me. He then led me into street evangelism in order that I might proclaim His message of love to passing crowds. Later I had the opportunity to proclaim God's Word through a weekly live radio broadcast that reaches several nations in West Africa. Having returned to the U.K. and taken up the pastorate of a small country church, we experienced a season of amazing church growth that enabled us to assist in the provision of aid for hundreds or even thousands of displaced people in Sierra Leone and Liberia.

You may ask, why tell this story? So that you can judge for yourself what I consider to be the amazing contemporary miracles God wrought in my life. My understanding of a miracle being an unexplainable or extraordinary event occurring without human planning or expectation, yet clearly identified as God's divine intervention. Because of the many extraordinary interventions I experienced, I have to accept that God still works miracles today. What I do not understand is why God chose me to experience such miraculous events, both in the United Kingdom and in West Africa. They were not things I looked for, prayed for, or even had great faith for. All I ever did was to go where God sent me, do as God instructed me, and proclaim what God gave me to say. I simply followed His instructions and directions the best I could and left Him to work the miracles.

Yet despite my experiences, I have always struggled with a poor self-image, which on many occasions has robbed me of peace and self-confidence. As Robert Kiyosaki wrote,

> *"It's not what you say out of your mouth that determines your life; it's what you whisper to yourself that has the most power!"*

Over the years, I have struggled with inner whispers of the night that remind me of my faults, failings, and weaknesses through which I find it so easy to put myself down. Even though there have been times when God has enabled me to speak His Word with power, those invasive whispers of the night would sometimes rob me of the assurance of God's peace and joy. Yet by God's grace, whenever I chose to do what I believed was God's will, the floodgates of heavenly resources were opened to the extent that I could not contain the blessings or the provision that God poured upon me and the resulting overflow became a blessing to many other people in many nations.

I pray you will enjoy my true story, but more importantly that you will encounter the God who inspired it. I know that many Christian people consider themselves as not being good enough for God but, as I have learnt to do, if they would just act in faith upon the Word of God that He is speaking into their lives rather than just react to their feelings, they also would be a blessing to many others. The faith I'm referring to is not so much having the belief that God exists; even the devil believes that! I'm referring to a faith that positively responds to the revealed Will of God in a person's life, regardless of their self-assessment. If we are willing to be what God wants us to be, to go where God wants us to go, and say what He wants us to proclaim – then one has to trust in Him—completely!

Chapter 1

A God Encounter

It was a typically cold and damp British winter's evening when, having spent most of the day in London waiting for a visa application to be processed, I was again compelled to wait in the shivering chill for a bus home to the village where I lived.

In my effort to stay warm whilst filling in time, I decided to walk around town for a bit of window shopping. Leaving the railway station, I walked down and into Reading's Market Square and noticed that Jackson's, the town's oldest department store, was still open. Attracted by its bright lights and thinking it would offer a warm place to wait for a while, I entered the store just to look around.

The men's section still had remnants of a recent sale with articles of clothing scattered over several tables with some having even fallen on the floor. I happily poked around this section for a while, searching for any last-minute bargains. Strangely, this store retained Reading's last remaining pneumatic tube cash system that provided a constant background swishing noise caused by the shuttles travelling inside the vacuum tubes conveying cash from various sales points to a cashier installed in the safety of some remote part of the building. The gentle swishing of the shuttles seemed to have a calming effect on me, and along with the relaxed atmosphere of the store, the pressure of the day concerning my fast-approaching trip to Africa began to lift.

Within a week, I had plans to visit Sierra Leone in West Africa, a country rapidly slipping into the grip of a diabolical civil war in which teenage bloodthirsty rebels were flooding into the country from Liberia. All the child rebels were forced to join various factions by other teenagers, who were their leaders. Kill or be killed was the rule for their lives. As a result, thousands of refugees, driven by fear and suffering unimaginable atrocities, were already fleeing in every possible direction from the bloodletting.

Now the time of the bus's departure was drawing close, and having found nothing suitable as gifts for my African friends, I began to make my way towards the exit of the store in preparation for a quick dash to the bus stop. Hesitating at the door for a moment or two, I fastened up the collar of my coat against the cold, damp air and stepped out onto King's Road.

As I took a few steps along the pavement before turning back into Market Square, I immediately lowered my head against the chilling wind. As I did so, a short African gentleman unexpectedly stood in front of me, seeming to be deliberately barring my way. Being forced to a stop, and thinking I hadn't seen him approaching, I began to apologise.

He, however, ignored my apology, stood his ground, and thrusting a small package up and into my face, he gruffly commanded, "Take this to Freetown."

I froze! It was immediately clear that this was not a chance encounter; this man, whoever he was, had intentionally stepped into my path to stop me. Somehow, he had known I had been in the store I hadn't even planned to visit. He must have been watching me, but from where and why? Being accosted in such an unexpected way was disconcerting, especially as it had been instigated by this unknown person on a busy Reading street.

Only my very closest friends knew of my plans to visit West Africa and carry significant funds on my person to aid my suffering African colleagues. This is why being accosted in such a challenging way was so startling. I had been caught totally off guard by his action and gruff demand.

For that reason, I was absolutely stunned that a total stranger knew both my whereabouts and my imminent travel plans. I must confess, rightly or wrongly, that I reacted to him by blurting out, "I'm not going to Freetown."

He, however, disregarded my protest and demanded for a second time that I take the package to Sierra Leone. I suppose I should have just walked away, but he continued to block my path whilst persisting with his demands.

Then, against every instinct for safety gained from travelling and living in West Africa for over thirty years, I engaged in conversation with him and inquired as to what was in the package. To this day, I do not know whether I made a very basic and stupid error, or whether this was a moment of divine intervention in preparation for what I can only say turned out to be a God appointment that He was literately pushing me into.

The response to the question I had just put to the gentleman was surprising. "It's a birthday present for the Commissioner of Police's son," he informed me. He continued to explain that he was the Police Commissioner's driver and had just purchased a birthday gift for the Commissioner's young son.

"Show me," I demanded.

So right there on the street, this unknown man from Africa unwrapped the gift he wanted me to carry, and with great care revealed a cheap, brightly painted tin car, the type that can be seen in any market stall.

I took it from him and examined it. It was, just as he said, a small tin car. Not knowing what else to do, I smelt the thing but was none the wiser for such a random act!

I then surprised myself by saying, "You can give me the toy car, but I may not take it to Africa, and I may choose to dispose of it."

He seemed happy enough with my response and handed the toy car over to me before disappearing into the gathering gloom of the evening, never to be seen by me again. Having missed my bus, I stood there for a while longer, feeling somewhat bemused over the whole unexpected event and then I started the long walk home.

Now, floods of questions began crowding my mind. Who was this man? How did he know I was in that store at that time? How long had he been waiting for me? And most vitally important, how did he know where I was going? Not one of these questions has ever been answered and the circumstances surrounding the encounter remain a mystery to me even to this day.

Only when I returned from West Africa did I come to understand that this strange encounter was God-ordained. Nevertheless, at that time I found the incident very disturbing and mysterious, for I had no way of knowing that every factor of this strange event was held safely in the hands of God.

During the time of this incident, the situation in Sierra Leone was seriously dangerous. The reports I had been receiving informed me that Liberian rebels had already infiltrated the city of Freetown, while other rebels were flooding across the international border from Liberia. Reports also indicated that hordes of these teenage rebels were travelling down through Sierra Leone committing horrendous crimes against humanity in which hundreds of Sierra Leoneans were being slaughtered and maimed. As a result of these incursions, many of my friends were telephoning from Africa, informing me of their imminent danger and their need for help, this being the reason for my visit.

At that time, I had moved on from the church and had returned to the building trade, where, through the generosity of many Christian friends, donations of aid were flooding into my office in support of the West African national Christians, resulting in my receiving large amounts of funds that I could share among my African colleagues during their time of dire need. The only way they could receive these funds was for me to carry them into West Africa on my person, which was why I did not want people to know I was visiting the war zones of Sierra Leone.

During my lifetime, I've learnt that God does not always choose the most religious people to do His will. In fact, as already mentioned, it is my observation that God chooses the weak, the foolish, and even the despised to accomplish His purposes. I also believe that those God calls, God also equips.

It is the people God equips whom He sends to accomplish His will. Such people are vital to His purposes. Even though many people may consider some of the things I have done to be foolish; I know that God has chosen me to accomplish these more unusual tasks, although I have absolutely no understanding why.

Everything about this encounter was unusual, unexplainable, or maybe even just plain foolish. I had just made a choice following this extraordinary encounter that would have been rejected by many a wiser Christian! I'm not trying to justify my actions, and to this day I still wonder how this event happened. I now have to live with unanswered questions concerning this event, yet I fully believe and accept that the encounter was ordained of God.

Within twenty-four hours of arriving in Sierra Leone, it became abundantly clear that God had chosen me for a very specific purpose. Although I was totally out of my depth, I was never beyond His protection and care, but at times I did have a few doubts. In case you are wondering, I did take an unwrapped toy car to Africa, which in my opinion, I could truthfully identify as being mine.

A few days after this strange encounter, I was on an uneventful flight into West Africa. I mention this because many times I have flown to the same destination in aircraft I will never set foot in again due to serious questions concerning their airworthiness. So, sitting back in the luxury of a VC10 British jet airliner was a great blessing.

The flight from London to Freetown took six hours and as the aircraft drew near its destination, I could sense that we were losing altitude. Looking down through my window, I could see the mighty Sierra Leone River flowing through the tropical jungle beneath me. As the aircraft continued to lose height, it made its customary pass diagonally across Lungi International Airfield, presumably to see if the runway was clear.

By now I could identify the giant cotton tree marking the airfield's boundary and noticed, thankfully, that the runway was clear of people, animals, and vehicles. But I was somewhat surprised to see several Nigerian or Mali warplanes parked in a corner of the airfield, presumably in readiness to bomb and strafe the rebels. Nigeria and Mali were supposedly part of an international peacekeeping force, established to protect the population of Sierra Leone and Liberia from the rebels. Their warplanes were used to bomb the rebels, but civilian villages were also bombed.

Once we landed, and because there were not as many disembarking passengers as normal, the race by all knowledgeable travellers to be the first to clear customs and immigration procedures did not occur. There was none of the normal pushing and shouting often encountered when entering this tropical airport. Nevertheless, I was still impacted and overwhelmed by the humidity and heat.

On this occasion, I sensed that there was a strange heavy atmosphere hanging over the airport, which subdued both airport officials and travellers alike. This unusual quietness was in stark contrast to the normal hubbub of the airport.

As is my custom, I travel with as little luggage as possible when visiting destinations in West Africa. As a rule, I never carry anything I am not willing or ready to leave behind, except for travel documents and currency, the latter having cost me many hours of argument and hassle with immigration, police, and army personnel, who were always very eager to relieve me of the burden of having to carry money on my person!

As always, I was glad to clear the so-called health check, along with immigration and customs procedures. Finally, upon entering the arrivals hall, I was greeted by my close friend and African brother, Richard. We bridged our cultures with a brief holding of hands according to his custom, thus confirming our friendship.

Thankfully, Richard had chartered the wreck of a yellow taxi to convey us from the airport to the ferry. The ferry provided the only way of reaching the city of Freetown as we had the Sierra Leone River to cross. On this occasion, we had to hurry to catch the last ferry of the day, so the taxi driver set off at an unnecessary speed, although it was quite a normal speed for a local taxi driver. He tended to drive on whatever side of the road he considered to be best.

We sped along the potholed road with the taxi horn blaring, causing women, children, and chickens to scatter from our pathway in the interest of protecting their lives whilst being covered in clouds of swirling African red dust. We passed through several hamlets where villagers earn a portion of their livelihood by selling fruit and articles from tiny market stalls situated alongside the road. Unfortunately, taxi drivers in their speeding vehicles rarely stopped to allow passengers to take a look or make a purchase, but the villagers lived in hope of having a customer.

It was almost dusk by the time we reached the ferry terminal where, as is normal in the tropics, the hot humid day would end suddenly with almost no twilight, when everything would be wrapped in darkness. Fortunately, we had arrived before the last ferry of the day left, for it was the only form of transport by which we could cross the five-mile-wide river. The loading procedures of these ferries always seem to take forever and are accompanied by much shouting and argument by anyone and everyone.

Crossing the river on board the ferry takes an hour or so, but as there is always so much activity on board, including some great palavers (animated local arguments), boredom is never a problem. Locally made snacks are available for those brave enough or sufficiently knowledgeable of what is safe for travellers to eat or drink.

By the time we reached Kissy Ferry Terminal on the city side of the river, night had fallen and it was intensely dark. The skill of the ferry pilot as he navigated his way against the incredibly strong river current was remarkable. He managed to dock alongside the terminal ramp without the aid of city lights, whilst at the same time avoiding several sunken vessels.

As always, it was with a sigh of relief that the weary travellers gratefully stepped off the ferry and onto dry ground. The ferry having docked, we walked over to collect Richard's vehicle which had been parked on a busy street near where the ferry is moored during the night. During Richard's absence, the car had been "guarded" by a youthful watchman, who for a small sum of money insisted that he would take good care of it. The fact that he would have damaged the car if he wasn't paid was also a consideration for paying for the protection offered!

Having left the terminal, we trundled slowly along the narrow streets of the city's East End towards the city centre. The night was still young, but the normally overcrowded streets were deserted due to strong rumours concerning the possibility of rebel infiltration. On that night, I became very aware that the strange close, humid, and silent heaviness, which I had noticed at the airport, was also hanging over the city. Throughout the unusual silence of the journey, we drove the city streets feeling that a hundred eyes were watching us, and there probably were!

Eventually, we reached the city centre without incident and drove up Siaka Stevens Street. We passed the banks, post office, and law courts and turned left at the giant cotton tree, which is an ancient landmark. Having turned onto Hill Station Road, we carefully skirted the Presidential State House, as we did not want to attract the attention of the presidential guards, and then almost immediately we turned into the car park of the Paramount Hotel that was once Freetown's premier hotel, amazingly, on this occasion, without hassle.

The security throughout that area was normally very tight. It was one of those places where many an unwary traveller had been stopped and forced to endure prolonged questioning and searches by security forces unless offering a monetary gift. In its better days, the Paramount was arguably the best hotel in the city. Unfortunately, neglect and rot had set in long ago and that night the damp stench of unkempt property hung heavily in the tropical air.

The sight of a couple of sad-looking prostitutes loitering with intent near the check-in desk gave me the feeling that I would rather not have been there. Arriving at the hotel desk, I was compelled to part with an amount in dollars that I felt was close to extortion in exchange for a night in a tatty dilapidated room. The room had only one benefit that I could discover, a lockable door. At least I felt safe for the night, even if I wasn't!

Sometimes daylight and bright sunshine change everything. The next morning, I opened the window of my stuffy room and was greeted with bird song along with the sounds of an awakening, but trafficless city.

Following a light breakfast, the only thing on offer, I set out to deliver the repackaged toy car to the Commissioner of Police. His office was located just a couple of blocks away from the hotel at police headquarters on George Street.

Feeling in a much better frame of mind than I had the previous evening, I walked the short distance towards his office with a lightness of heart. On the way, I passed the city fountain, which had never worked even though it was constructed by a friend of mine. As always, I kept as far away as possible from the State House guards, knowing I would be detained if I got too close.

Passing the cotton tree on my left, I glanced over towards the American Embassy to ensure it was open, as it offered the only safe place to which I could run in the event of trouble. Standing next to the great cotton tree, I could see police headquarters and noticed several armed police casually standing around its entrance.

I approached them carefully, and thankfully, they appeared to be relaxed and at ease. They were friendly enough as they inquired into my business and were very curious and particularly interested concerning my mission on behalf of the commissioner's driver, whom they knew. Their curiosity was especially heightened due to there being very few white people walking the streets of the city at that time.

Having a little knowledge of Creole, the local street language, I attempted to communicate with them in a way that helped identify me as someone familiar with local customs. Then, having explained my situation, I offered the package to them, requesting that they pass it on to the Commissioner.

My request was immediately and bluntly refused, but in accordance with local custom, I was invited to hand the package to the Commissioner myself.

Responding to their invitation, I followed them into the building where I was handed over to a second group of military security guards. Sullenly and with their automatic guns swinging loosely at their sides, they promptly marched me up the stairs to the top floor of the four-story building.

Having reached the Commissioner's office, I was confronted by a contingency of elite guards armed with submachine guns. These no-nonsense military personnel had known active service and were loyal to the President. The friendly atmosphere with which I had been greeted at the door of the building had now totally dissipated as these guards demanded to know my business.

I showed them the now-reopened package containing the toy car and informed them of my mission. I requested that they pass it on to the Commissioner. Suddenly and without warning, their response to my request was to unlock the Commissioner's office door and forcefully thrust me inside. The door was then immediately and firmly closed and locked behind me.

Feeling more trapped than welcomed, I looked around the office and it seemed huge. Although the room was unoccupied, the air conditioning was blasting out cooled air, causing the office to feel extremely cold. Soon I began to shiver, although by this time there were possibly other reasons for my shivering!

Towards the rear of the office were several spacious armchairs set around a coffee table. At the business end of the office stood an impressive mahogany desk upon which papers and maps had been scattered haphazardly. It seemed obvious to me that the papers had recently been studied, presumably by the Commissioner, and judging from the way the papers had been scattered, it seemed that he had left the room on very short notice.

As I looked over the desk, my eye caught the title of an open folder, causing me to immediately feel considerably uncomfortable. Being disturbed by what I had just seen, I looked for a way out of the office but, having been locked in, I discovered there was no way of escape. The reason for my concern and wanting to remove myself immediately from the office was the title of the folder. Written in large capital red letters were the words, "Top Secret - For your eyes only - Rebel incursion into Sierra Leone."

I turned and walked thoughtfully towards the windows. Looking down onto George Street several floors below, I wondered if there was another way out of the office. I recalled that only a few weeks previously, a man had supposedly "jumped" to his death from these very windows, and now I was wondering why!

At that moment I did the only thing possible left for me to do—I lifted my heart to God and offered a strange prayer: "Lord," I prayed. "What am I doing here, at this time, and in this place? Please help me."

I recalled the chance encounter I had had with the man in Reading, the reluctant decision I made to carry the package for him, the forceful way I had just been pushed into the Commissioner's office, the locked and guarded door preventing my exit, and the extremely sensitive papers scattered all over the Commissioner's desk. The only thing I could do was to sit in the chair that was furthest away from the desk, pray, and wait.

It seemed an interminable age before a previously unnoticed door burst open and the Commissioner swept into the room. He was a portly gentleman of short stature with perspiration rolling down his face in rivulets, maybe from the tropical heat or whatever problem he has just encountered. He had stridden halfway across his office before noticing me and when he did, he stopped abruptly. For a moment or two he just stared at me. He then took a long look at his desk with open papers scattered over it and looked back at me.

It seemed to me that he was undecided as to what to do next. Recognising that this was not a moment for indecision or waiting to see what he would do, I jumped to my feet and knowing he was a Muslim, I proclaimed, "Sir, I am a servant of Jesus Christ. I know you are under great stress; I have come to pray for you."

Silence filled the room as he contemplated what I had just said. He continued to look between me and the sensitive papers and during those moments, time seemed to freeze. Then very slowly, he began to walk over to his desk and having reached his chair, he slowly sank into its plush comfort. After a moment or two, he looked up and quietly said, "Please pray for me."

I moved over and knelt beside him. Placing my hand on his shoulder, I began to pray. I have to confess that it was a very long prayer that included most of the gospel message as it pertains to Jesus and His love. But before I reached the "amen" bit of the prayer, the office door once again burst open and in strode a uniformed woman covered in gold braid. She was obviously a woman on a mission.

Seeing me on my knees next to the Commissioner, she abruptly stopped and stared. This high-ranking officer was clearly taking some time to evaluate the unusual scene confronting her. In the following silence, it seemed to me that my situation was deteriorating, so I decided to continue praying audibly for the Commissioner for the benefit of the Assistant Commissioner whilst offering an inner silent prayer to God for help!

Having concluded my prayer, the following silence was electrifying. Suddenly and unexpectedly, the Assistant Commissioner burst out in her deep African voice, uttering, "Amen Lord, amen!" For a moment or so, silence once again descended. She then began to speak very slowly and deliberately saying, "I have been praying for this man for many years; help him, Lord Jesus, help him."

In God's providence the Assistant Commissioner, who was also the leader of the local Church of Salvation, accepted this amazing moment as being ordained of God. The atmosphere in the office immediately relaxed.

Having risen from my knees, I handed the cheap tin car over to the Commissioner, who now seemed to accept me as his friend. We then chatted together for a while longer before I took my leave.

Once I was outside and clear of the police headquarters, I stopped to ponder the unexpected events that had just transpired, realising that the whole encounter had been planned by God from the very moment I was confronted on a busy Reading Street right through to praying with the Commissioner in his office at his moment of great crisis. To me, this whole event was miraculous for it had been orchestrated by God Himself.

A few days later, I received news that President Momoh had imprisoned the Commissioner within the notorious Pademba Road Prison for failing to prevent the rebel incursion. Although there were many rumours, I am unaware of what eventually happened to the Commissioner. What I am sure about is that within these unexpected and unexplainable events, God wanted that man to hear about Jesus and to be prayed for during his time of great need. I just happened to be a little cog within the great purposes of God, who had ordained that a "chance" meeting on a Reading Street would result in praying with the Police Commissioner of Sierra Leone. What a privilege— what a miracle!

Chapter 2
A Failed Christian Is Rescued

Born on October 31, 1941, just a few years before World War II ended, I still retain memories of the war's final days. As a small boy living in the South of England adjacent to the garrison town of Aldershot, I would be excited when woken up at night by the unique droning of Lancaster and Wellington bombers flying low over my house as they returned to their base just a few miles away following their bombing raids. On occasion, I would push back my blanket, crawl to the end of the bed, kneel at the windowsill, and search for them in the night sky.

They were always difficult to see as they flew without lights, but sometimes I could make out their shadowy shapes in the moonlight. All around me there were great fingers of light reaching up into the night sky, as operatives sought enemy planes with their searchlights. Amid all this excitement, I could also hear the distinctive sound of Spitfires and Hurricanes as the little fighter planes crisscrossed overhead defending the bombers as they returned from their bombing raids and nearby military installations.

Even though the war ended on May 8, 1945, life remained challenging, as it did for most families like mine. Government orders instructed us to continue practising sheltering in a safe place when the air-raid sirens sounded just in case there was a surprise aircraft attack.

In our house, the safe place was deemed to be under the staircase. It was a very confined place where our gas meter was located. So, we would sit on the gas meter and practice putting on the gas mask! How I hated that gas mask—the smell of it was awful and it was very tight-fitting, making it uncomfortable to wear.

Food shortages continued for several years after the war, which meant that sometimes our meal of the day would consist of just a slice or two of bread toasted over a small fire. On these occasions, we sat around the fire and constantly turned our slices of bread on the toasting fork until they turned golden brown. When toasted to perfection, we covered it with dripping, or the residue fat left in a container after meat has been cooked in it. The toast and dripping tasted so good that we always asked for more.

On rare occasions, and as a very special treat, I was entrusted with the family's ration book that allowed me to purchase a few pennies' worth of boiled sweets when visiting the local newsagents, but only when one of my parents was standing beside me to ensure I didn't overspend my allowance. Little did I understand that my hard-working parents, along with most other parents at that time, faced serious financial challenges. There were times I would find my mother in tears, having to explain to the rent man that she was unable to pay the week's rent.

Many of the clothes I wore were second-hand. One of my greatest of all childhood embarrassments was having to wear sturdy brown second-hand women's shoes to primary school. I couldn't hide these shoes from the other boys I played with on the playground, but who cared anyway? At least we had a ball to kick. Being a slow learner, I disliked school and can recall the frequent rappings I received across my knuckles from teachers who I assumed didn't like me.

Eventually, at age eleven, I moved on to a local secondary school where I was eventually encouraged by the headmaster to leave the educational system altogether at age fourteen. I continued to live at home where my parents immediately sent me to work. As was the custom of the day, most of my salary, around one pound sterling a day, was surrendered to my parents to help towards the family budget. Today, I very much regret wasting those educational years, knowing, as the headmaster wrote on my final school report, "Could have done better." How right he was!

During my early childhood, my father worked in his family's market garden business. I would sometimes walk over the fields to watch him plough and cultivate the land with the help of a huge horse named Drummer, but I always thought it was named "Dumber."

A few years later, having left the family business, both my father and my mother experienced a religious awakening. They subsequently became Christian children's evangelists. From that day on, Father toured the south of England with a marquee, holding evangelistic campaign meetings for children in many of England's rural villages. Even at the age of around ten years, I was expected to help with the erecting and setting up of the marquee, digging latrines, and participating in all the Christian activities organised by my parents. I was supposed to be an example of how a fifties Christian child should live and act. Unfortunately, I fell well short of that example, much to the exasperation of my parents.

As part of my enforced Christian commitment, I was compelled to attend chapel twice every Sunday, participate in all the activities of Christian youth meetings, read my Bible every day, and say a prayer before going to bed. Real kids' stuff, like scouting or playing football, was strictly forbidden, along with all other forms of so-called worldly entertainment, such as the cinema.

As time passed, I longed to be free from all parental constraints, for I craved the same excitement and adventures that many of my school friends talked about.

I can recall that my parents, who were adherents of the Plymouth Brethren movement, believed they were called of God to be "children's evangelists." Consequently, they joined a missionary society and from then on, they lived by faith (a religious term for being unwaged). As such, there were times when we as a family were compelled to live in exceedingly impoverished conditions, especially when there was not enough money to put food on the table.

During these times, my parents were forced to go hungry whilst my sister and I would eat whatever food was left in the house. It was during those days when being subjected to a strict religious upbringing that I began to develop a deep resentment against all things Christian or religious. To my embarrassment, whilst attending secondary school, I discovered that I had been circumcised, presumably on the eighth day. It was a ritual, which gratefully, I do not remember happening. However, the evidence of this ritual became a problem to me when taking showers following sports sessions at school when other classmates notice this sort of thing.

Because I was forbidden to mix with non-Christian boys of my own age, I became a bit of a loner. Unfortunately, as such, I developed some very sneaky habits that were kept hidden from my parents. I have since discovered that sneakiness, unless dealt with, becomes a lifetime habit causing difficulties in other relationships.

Nevertheless, despite my rebellious feelings and sneaky attitude, I was baptised into the Christian faith at the age of eleven. Then, according to the prescribed teaching of the day, I was permitted to take communion every Sunday morning. From that day on, I was expected to read my Bible and say a prayer every night when kneeling at my bedside. Yet all this was done without my ever really encountering or knowing the God who loved me. Looking back, I now know that I grew up in an enforced religious ritual that for me was devoid of a personal relationship with God.

When I reached my early teens, I was still compelled to assist my parents with the hard physical "God work" they were involved with. During mandatory family prayer times, I would deliberately block my ears against the fervent prayers being made and by now I had become bored with reading the Bible, something I was compelled to do. My rejection of my parents' faith had now morphed into a resentment against all things Christian, from which I sought to escape. I suppose by this time I would clearly have been identified as a rebel.

I now realise that the seeds of rebellion were evident in my life from quite an early age. I understand that my attitude towards school authorities was foolish, as my exasperated teachers resorted to caning me for correctional purposes. Then in earnest desperation, they sent me to the headmaster, who supported their action by repeating the punishment. If my father happened to hear of these events, he endorsed the school's actions with a third beating. Partly due to the triple administration of corrective punishment, I learned never to share any of my misadventures with my parents, which consequently deepened my alienation from the family.

When, at the age of fourteen with only the most minimal education, I was encouraged by the headmaster to leave school, it did not take long for me to discover that my wasted years of education had now become a major stumbling block in advancing in any career opportunity I sought. The outcome was that I drifted from one dull manual employment to another.

My first occupation was as a labourer hired to cut grass and hedges around an orchard by hand. Sometimes, old school friends passing by would laugh and joke about my employment. Later, when offered work in a small market garden, I was required to labour eight hours a day at the backbreaking task of weeding vegetable and root crops, such as carrots and lettuce, by hand and often on my knees. The only rest from this soul-destroying occupation was preparing the occasional chicken for sale at the local market.

A few years later, when offered the opportunity to work as an under-gardener on a beautiful private estate, I didn't hesitate to accept the opportunity.

During those years, although I was responsible for maintaining the property and grounds of my parents that were used for Christian activities, my lifestyle was causing great tensions in the family, so when offered employment as a cowman, which required my moving out of the family home and living on the farm where I would be working, I was encouraged to accept the employment. For a while, everyone was happy.

As far as I was concerned, I was free now aged eighteen. I purchased my first motorbike and thought that at last, I had gained my freedom! Gratefully, I have since discovered that there is a vital difference between being compelled to be religious and choosing to live in a relationship with God. For me, being religious suggests a somewhat negative lifestyle that forbids a person from participating in activities classified as "worldly." Although I had left home and had rejected even my limited understanding of God, hindsight reveals that God had never abandoned or rejected me. His hand was still upon me, even though I never knew it.

In my mind, I was now the son my father never had! I had been replaced by his "spiritual sons," some of whom I deeply resented. For me, my religious past was to be forgotten and I now assumed that I was free to do as I chose. Although I would not admit it at the time, I confess that my attitude towards my parents and other special people in my life was the cause of broken relationships, a damaged reputation, and intense heartbreak, all of which I now regret.

Having made some big mistakes, I was about to discover that the wonderful God in heaven was not willing to let me drift into the devil's hands completely. His hand was still upon me, and I can categorically state that God in His grace brought me through those difficult years until I encountered a life-changing experience. This encounter occurred, appropriately, in the town of Gravesend in Kent, for it was there that my old lifestyle was buried and where I chose to be baptised.

I abandoned employment on the farm when offered an opportunity for a substantial increase in salary by being employed as an "improver" in the plastering trade. The opportunity to move into the building trade was made possible through the generosity of a very old Christian gentleman, who at one time had owned a leading building company. He knew my parents and the problems I had caused; yet when he heard I was seeking employment, he provided me with a suitable opportunity. He even offered me a room in his own home.

I was soon to learn that my benefactor, Mr Hopkins, or Uncle Hoppy as he was affectionately known, was so totally committed to God that he had distributed all his wealth to Christian mission organisations. It was his habit to rise at six every morning and pray for missions and the people he knew until breakfast time. He was incredibly near-sighted, which resulted in him bumping into everything and everybody; yet that man knew how to pray. He would pray until he saw the hand of God move with power in the lives of those he cared for, and that included me.

The previous occupant of the room Uncle Hoppy offered me was a Christian known by thousands as Brother Andrew. He was the remarkable Dutchman who achieved great things for God as recorded in his book, *God's Smuggler*.

The outcome of my occupying that room was that I met the same God whom both Uncle Hoppy and Brother Andrew knew, and whom I was running away from!

A few months after moving in with Uncle Hoppy, I received an invitation from my father to attend a Christian meeting to be held on the other side of the River Thames in the town of Grays in Essex, where he was booked to be the preacher. At that time, there was a ferry linking Gravesend to Grays, so having reluctantly agreed to attend the meeting, due to my past attitudes to him, I took the ferry across the river on the appropriate Saturday afternoon. Later that evening whilst attending the Christian meeting, I unexpectedly met with God, or should I say, God met with me. Throughout the service, the Holy Spirit brought me under a deep conviction of sin and my rebellious attitude towards my family and the many people who cared about me. This resulted in me leaving the meeting that evening greatly disturbed.

Night had fallen by the time I returned to Gravesend. Still disturbed by the events of the evening, I stood on the upper deck of the green-painted ferry and stared down at the dark swirling waters racing beneath me. The River Thames, being a tidal river between its mouth at the sea and London city, was now in full flood and on that dark night it gave me the feeling that my life, like the waters beneath me, was racing away into the unknown darkness. In desperation, I took the cigarette I was smoking from my mouth and flicked it away. I watched as it spun away until suddenly it was swallowed up by the dark waters.

As it disappeared into the blackness, I cried out, "God, if you're there, help me." At that moment, feeling that my life was also spinning away out of control into an unknown blackness, I turned to God.

In His grace, He heard my cry for help and later that night as I knelt beside my bed, the Spirit of God wrestled with my soul as I envisioned my rebellious life being swallowed up by the unknown darkness surrounding me.

Following that encounter, I retired to my room early the next several evenings. I had no appetite for the normal activities of a young man. I would kneel beside my bed with a Bible before me and pray.

I remember, as clearly as though it was only yesterday, the evening when, waiting before God, the presence and power of the Holy Spirit suddenly fell upon me. I immediately came under a great conviction of sin concerning my wasted life. Then, before the throne of God, I began confessing all the rebellion, foolishness and wasted opportunities of my past life in an act of repentance.

As I sensed the convicting truth of God resting upon me, the Holy Spirit searched through all my foolishness as I wept with regret. Suddenly, having made full confession of all the wrongs I had committed, the presence of the Holy Spirit changed from convicting me to comforting me. At that moment I began to experience wave after wave of forgiveness as the cleansing power of God flooded over me again and again and again. It seemed that every area of my life was being washed and renewed by God Himself.

Much later that evening, having risen from my knees, I knew I was a new man through the grace and power of God.

Returning to work the next day, my work colleagues immediately noticed the transformation in my life. Just a few days later, a work colleague took hold of me and began shaking me as he shouted, "Swear at me, swear at me! I don't know who you are anymore. You have changed!"

He did not understand that God had removed all forms of blasphemy from my heart and mouth. To my shame, I confess that a few days later, having sustained a head injury on a metal pole, I did utter an exasperated oath. Every worker within earshot of my voice stopped and looked at me, expressing their surprise. I think they were as disappointed at this temporary breakdown in my reformed lifestyle as I was.

Being somewhat heartbroken over this incident, I immediately sought God for forgiveness. Even today, I remain amazed at the transformation that only God could have accomplished in my life. He even removed the craving for nicotine, which I hadn't noticed until a few weeks later when I discovered half a packet of cigarettes in my coat pocket. I immediately threw the packet away. What an amazing God we have, and He loves us so much.

I just love this verse from the Bible: *"When anyone is joined to Christ, he is a new being; the old is gone, the new has come. All this is done by God, who through Christ changed us from enemies into his friends and gave us the task of making others his friends also"* 2 Corinthians 5:17-18. How true this verse is—and how accurate.

With hindsight, I now know that although surrounded by sincere religious activity, I had never understood or discovered what a true relationship with "the God of the Bible" was all about. Yet that was the God who, in the days to come, was going to accomplish remarkable and miraculous events in my life.

Everything changed for me following an encounter with this God over several days in my early twenties. Through that encounter, I experienced a total transformation of life! The outcome was, as the Bible puts it, that I was born again by the power of the Holy Spirit.[1] It wasn't so much that I came to accept the religion of my parents; rather it was an occasion when I encountered the life-changing power of God. Through that amazing encounter, all the sham and shame of my past was dealt with through God's amazing grace. Then, as I journeyed through acts of repentance and confession, I was embraced by God's peace and love.

From the very first moment of that God encounter, I began to live a new life through the grace of God. It was through the power of the Holy Spirit that my life was transformed. Since that spiritual encounter, God has led me from one adventure to the next. I confess that sometimes the events in my life have been a bit challenging, or even disappointing when I got things wrong, yet the God who has done such great things in my life continues to help me, which is nothing short of miraculous.

Today, I can state with total conviction that since the day that God in heaven placed His hand upon me, my life has totally changed. I am fully persuaded that:

> God's grace is greater than all my faults and failings.
>
> God's love covers all my sins and weaknesses.
>
> God's protection defends me from dangers seen and unseen.
>
> God's purpose for my life cannot be thwarted, for with Him nothing is impossible.
>
> God's provision overwhelms all my impoverishment for He supplies my every need.

---

1   John 3:3-8.

Chapter 3

Nothing Is Impossible with God

As time slipped by, my hunger for God and His Word increased. I was now attending a lively church where great friendships were being forged with people around my own age. I discovered one friend, who was a great encourager to me. His name was Robin and we spent much of our free time together, including attending youth meetings, special events, and parties, into which he was a great gate-crasher.

Due to unforeseen circumstances, I hadn't seen Robin for a while as I needed to support my mother and father back in their home. Father had unexpectedly become seriously ill and was in hospital, where he was not expected to recover, whilst my mother was struggling to manage on her own.

Nevertheless, I was very eager to share with Robin a remarkable God intervention that had occurred in my life concerning a choice I had to make about applying to a Bible college for missionary training.

A few weeks previous to my father's illness, I had been asked to take a visiting missionary to a special missionary meeting he was to speak at in a small chapel deep within the Kentish countryside. He had recently returned from North Africa and was not sure how to find his way to this appointment. Having driven him to the little chapel deep within a very remote country area, I was able to watch his illustrated presentation, including his photographs of life in the Sahara Desert.

His talk centred upon the nomadic Tuareg people of the Sahara, sometimes known as "the mysterious blue people." One of his photographs became so etched in my memory that I committed myself to pray daily for this particular group of desert Tuareg people.

Eventually, after several months of praying for the Tuaregs, I inquired of God, saying, "Lord, do you want me to do more than just pray for these people? Do you want me to support the missionaries who are seeking to reach these Tuareg people with the gospel of Jesus in any way?" My idea was that I would visit the Sahara Desert in the capacity of a handyman, where I would be willing to maintain, repair, and paint the houses of the missionaries. In my thinking, they would then be free to do the real missionary work like preaching and teaching.

With a strong sense of divine prompting, I began making inquiries as to how to contact the missionary whose slide show I had seen. After some time, it became clear that I would have to write him a letter— something I dreaded doing!

Due to my having a wasted education, it took me several hours to compose, write, and then rewrite what I considered to be a letter suitable for this situation. As was normal in those days, I had to purchase an airmail letter form from the post office on which my letter could be written. Having made the purchase, I diligently and ponderously copied my message onto the airmail letter form. It was a challenging task but having completed it, I then discovered that I did not have an address to send it to! However, the missionary had clearly said that he lived in the middle of the Sahara Desert. So, taking him at his word and taking a very practical handyman's approach to the problem, I looked for an atlas and began searching for the Sahara Desert.

I eventually found it in Africa, and the desert looked enormous! Nevertheless, again taking the missionary at his word when he said he was living in a town in the centre of the desert, I took a ruler and pencil and measured the desert from left to right, then from top to bottom and marked what was the approximate centre.

I noticed that the nearest town to my mark was Tamanrasset. So in my simplicity, I addressed my airmail letter form with the missionary's name and his mission, and added Tamanrasset, Sahara Desert, Africa! In the letter, I offered support in the role of a handyman to help maintain the properties. Taking the letter to the local post box, I posted it. Ten days later I received a reply! The response provided the first step on a long and challenging journey in which I was going to experience the life-changing grace and power of God, to whom nothing is impossible.

In his reply letter, the missionary instructed me to apply for a training course at Emmanuel Bible College, Birkenhead, UK. Having complied with his instructions by writing to the college, I received a comprehensive response within a few days. Enclosed with their reply were many forms with questions I found impossible to answer. It took several weeks for me to find friends who could help me answer those questions. Eventually, thanks to the help of many friends, the challenging task was completed, and the forms were returned to the college.

The closing date for all applications was clearly marked as being mid-June, and it was already mid-August. So before posting my application, I prayed, "Lord, I will only attend this Bible college if the principal and staff conclude it is Your will for me to do so." A few days later, I received a reply from the college which concluded, "You may attend the course if you believe it is God's will for you to do so."

What a dilemma. I just did not know what to do, for the final choice of attending or not attending the college had been firmly placed back into my hands!

The only person I knew as someone who could help me at such a time as this was my friend Robin. We were very close and he had already been a great help to me in my Christian life, so I decided to seek his counsel.

At the time, I was living in Basingstoke, supporting my father and mother, while Robin was still living in Gravesend. Having called Robin on the telephone, I made arrangements to visit him the following week, knowing that we would pray and together seek God's will concerning this important issue of my attending a Bible college, something that Robin himself was very keen to do.

The following Saturday afternoon, I travelled by train to Gravesend and took a local bus to the street where he lived. Walking from where the bus had stopped, I arrived at his house but uncharacteristically, I hesitated at his gate due to an inner reluctance to approach the front door. Three times I walked up to his gate, only to pass by. This was ridiculous—why was I doing this when normally I would be calling out his name in greeting as I approached the front door of his house?

Eventually, his mother saw me through her kitchen window and came bursting out of the house, shouting, "How did you know? How did you know?" As it was, I *didn't* know!

She then managed to tearfully inform me of the tragic news she had just received from the police. Robin, along with his girlfriend, had just lost their lives on one of Britain's busiest motorways, M2, in a car accident, and she hadn't even had the time to inform the other members of the family, which is why she was so amazed to see me.

Having spent some time with her as we grieved together, I returned to my home that evening broken-hearted and angry. I told God that it was Robin who wanted to go to Bible college rather than myself and that He should have allowed Robin to do so. That evening, in the solitude of my bedroom, I poured out my emotional thoughts and feelings to God in prayer.

Wonderfully and graciously, God responded to my prayers as the Holy Spirit led me to the Scriptures which read, *"Do not say, 'I am only a boy;' for you shall go to all to whom I send you"* Jeremiah 1:7 NRSV. Those words reached deep into the inner recesses of my heart, and I knew God was speaking to me even as I read the Scriptures. This was all I needed to go ahead and inform the college that I knew it was God's will for me to attend the Bible college, and within ten days I arrived at the Emmanuel Bible College.

My sister and future brother-in-law had kindly offered to drive me in their car on the 150-mile journey to the college. Unfortunately, the old car suffered a breakdown, and it took so long to repair that we arrived at the college very late. By the time we reached there, the new intake of students was already integrating into college life. I was somewhat rebuked by the principal for my late arrival, but he provided us with some refreshments after our challenging journey.

Our late arrival and time spent with the principal caused our introductions and initial interaction with the other students to be very minimal. I noticed that they particularly engaged easily with my sister's fiancé, whilst my speech and dress identified me more as a labourer in the building trade rather than a potential student. The outcome was that the very few conversations I engaged in were minimal and very polite.

All too soon the time came for my sister and future brother-in-law's departure, at which point the entire student body came over to me and said goodbye, wishing me a safe journey home. A very strange quietness descended on the gathered assembly when they were informed that I was the one staying and it was my companion who was leaving!

I can only say that college life was a major challenge to me, and I was later informed that I was a particular challenge to the faculty staff! Having to adjust to lectures, academic studies, dress code, and a new lifestyle was all somewhat alien to my free spirit. I do, however, have great admiration for the college staff, who accepted me as someone who was happier with a sledgehammer in his hand than a pen.

Although I lost body weight during the first year, the college gained many improvements to its buildings. By God's grace, I completed the two-year course and graduated with a college diploma. In my second year, I was also given the Student of the Year award, which seemed to shock my fellow students and it certainly did me, for the principal had to call my name twice before I responded.

As amazing as my graduation from college was to all who knew me, I learnt a greater personal lesson. During those college years, I learnt that God never makes a mistake in a person's life. Although it was very tough to adjust to college life, I learnt that where God leads, God also teaches, equips, and supplies every need in a person's life—for the body, mind, and spirit. For with God, nothing, and I mean absolutely nothing, is impossible.

My recent experiences, including meeting the missionary I took to his missionary meeting, seeing the photos of the Tuareg tribespeople whom I prayed for every day, and volunteering to maintain mission property in various places in the Sahara Desert, had changed me. After a short course in car maintenance in a local garage belonging to a Christian proprietor, I was on my way to Algeria.

Chapter 4
Encountering God in the Sahara

The French-built SE-210 Caravelle, on which I was flying from Paris to Algiers, was my first flight on a jet airliner. The atmosphere on board was very relaxed, allowing the air hostesses to sit back and chat with each other, for there were very few passengers on board.

Flying high over the Mediterranean Sea gave me ample opportunity for contemplation of what the future might hold. I was feeling a touch of strangeness now that I had passed the point of no return. Behind me were friends, supporters, and my old lifestyle; before me was the great unknown in a land still recovering from the violence of civil war.

All too soon, the aircraft began its descent for what was to be my first visit to the great continent of Africa. As we flew low over the city of Algiers, I could clearly see dazzling white buildings clustered around the harbour, with city streets stretching up and into the surrounding horseshoe-shaped foothills of the Atlas Mountains.

The aircraft, having swung away from the towering mountain, then settled into its final approach. We passed over vineyards stretching out alongside the Mediterranean Sea, then over the local Hippodrome, where local horse and trap racing takes place, and finally touched down on the runway. I had now arrived in Africa for the very first time.

Disembarking from the plane, I approached the immigration officers, who were perched in raised passport booths from where they could look down upon arriving passengers.

The officer in the booth I had selected peered down at me sullenly, his face anything but friendly. Communication with him was difficult as I had no knowledge of French and, even if he understood English, he was not willing to use it. Eventually, however, he stamped my passport that granted me a three-month visitor's visa. From there I made my way through to where the customs desks are located, collected my case, passed through the doors and entered a huge public reception hall.

By this time, I was very grateful to be greeted by a former Emmanuel Bible College student, who was waiting for me. Although we had attended the same Bible college for two years, I had never spoken to her apart from a formal "Yes, sister" or "No, sister." Emmanuel, being part of the holiness movement, had forbidden communication between male and female students! It all felt a bit strange as we sat in the back of a taxi, enjoying our first conversation, although we had known each other for more than two years.

The taxi, having taken us through the fascinating city of Algiers, arrived at the Christian guest house where I would be staying. Dar Nama, as the house was named, had been built high up on the encircling hills overlooking the city and commanded a great view of the surrounding area.

The building was of Moorish design, typically protected by high walls containing a strong solid wooden arched gate. Entering the property was like walking out of one world and into another. Once through the gate, all the heat and dust, along with an endless hooting of cars forcing their way through a confusion of bustling streets, were left behind. Upon entering the property, I immediately stepped out of the hustle and bustle of the city and into a tranquil and cool outer courtyard shaded by fig trees that surrounded a central pool boasting a fountain. It felt a bit like something from an old movie!

Having been welcomed and greeted by the host, who was an energetic, soft-spoken man, I was led into the quaint inner building with its narrow staircases and twisted corridors.

Eventually, I was shown to a room at the back of the property containing its own tiny kitchen facility, which I could use.

After a couple of days of settling in, I was supposed to give all my time to learning Algerian Arabic from a French textbook. I found this a little challenging as I had no knowledge of French, but as I was now a real missionary, I got on with the task as best I could without complaint, well, maybe not too many complaints!

Fortunately, a youngish British missionary named Maurice offered to help me from time to time. Sometimes he would take me out into the city where we would venture into many of its interesting areas.

On one occasion, we visited a vast housing estate in which two flats had been transformed into an inner-city monastery. The twelve priests living there were adherents of the Little Brothers of Jesus, a sect of the Roman Catholic church founded by Charles de Foucauld. De Foucauld had lived among the Tuareg people of the Sahara Desert during the 1900s when he was assassinated in his hermitage.

It was the practice of these twelve followers of de Foucauld, for six of them to seek employment with which they supported the other six, who had given themselves to full-time study and prayer. Apparently, they exchanged roles every six months.

Before we left, we prayed together. I found this experience both interesting and challenging, for not only were they the first desert missionaries I met, but they also practised silent prayer. I found it very difficult to know when to add my amen.

In due course, the leader of my mission arrived back from the UK, bringing an end to my daily extended walks. He made it very clear that I should give much greater attention to language study. This involved me sweating over the task of learning Arabic every day alone in my room. Unfortunately, the mission leader found me to be something of a challenge and once described me as "the shaft of a spear that needed to be polished before use!" I never did discover what he was implying by having me polished.

Sometime later, he dispatched me on an eighteen-hour bus journey to the desert town of Touggourt, where I would be out of his way for a while. Normally, the rented property where I would be living was used by the midwives of the mission, but as they were all afflicted with hepatitis, I had the property to myself.

All Christian mission activity was and is forbidden in Algeria, including in the Sahara Desert. Christians can enter Algeria in the capacity of their professions, in this case as midwives. I was able to remain in Algeria on a tourist visa, which meant leaving the country every three months and renewing the visa when I returned. I would normally visit Morocco or Tunisia to renew my visitor visa.

From the first day, I loved the desert! The house I was staying in was built with sun-baked mud bricks and located within sight of the town's centre. As with every other property, it had an accessible flat roof, where I would spend most of my time, except during the hottest parts of the day. Importantly for me, it was located close to the local coffee shop. From the roof of the house, I could view most of the town, but even more excitingly, when looking south over the desert sands, which stretched away for mile after mile, I could see in the distance an area known as the "great whispering dunes." Most evenings around sundown, as I gazed across the desert to the dunes, they would be covered with a breath-taking glory of colours from a gentle blush of pink that slowly morphed into deep reds and purples as the sun set behind them. On the occasions when moderate winds whipped up the sands, the whole surrounding western horizon was filled with the glow of an evening sunset.

Most nights, I chose to sleep on the roof of the house under the stars. Every night I required four blankets which, having been shaken to ensure there were no scorpions lurking in them, I would pull over me one by one as the night temperature dropped. I never wanted to miss an opportunity to search the heavens, for they contained the glory of God in ways I have never seen before or since.

Some nights, the stars appeared to be so close that it seemed I could almost reach up and touch them. Memories of that desert place will remain forever in my mind.

Most days I would rise around 5:30 a.m. It was then my normal practise to frequent the local coffeehouse where I sat at a table with a cup of very strong local coffee, served in the smallest of all coffee cups with lumps of sugar almost the same size as the cup, and watch the sunrise. It was always a magnificent sight as the sun ascended but, in many ways, it was different from the evening sunset.

But the moment the tip of the sun could be seen rising above the desert sands, my hand would be covered in flies. What a challenge those flies were! They were everywhere and into everything, millions of the wretched things that immediately covered everything. I never did discover what kept them alive in that vast barren and waterless expanse of desert.

Then, as the temperature climbed steadily throughout the morning, my life was lived in any patch of shade that could be found.

The people I met around the town were hospitable. Sometimes in the evening, having finished my daily shopping for food, I was invited to a game of chess or draughts in one of the local all-male cafés. I never won a game, and I'm not sure I wanted to, for these were hardy men. My opponent would normally be assisted with a steady stream of advice from all of the cafe's customers. They were friendly enough, but I took care never to be offensive; I was just happy to play the game, having already decided that winning was not necessary.

I have to confess that I am a terrible language student. My tutorial book gave little or no understanding of the correct pronunciations of the language I was supposedly learning. However, in the early evenings, the night watchman, who normally slept outside the house on his mat, would allow me to sit with him on the street. He displayed unlimited patience in his efforts to teach me his native language.

Towards the end of my time there, I was just beginning to understand him. Yet whilst living in the desert, there was a voice I did hear and over time, came to recognise with some clarity. It was the voice of the Holy Spirit. He did not speak to me audibly but rather with an inner voice that illuminated the Scriptures with which I spent many hours. This led to an experience that made my time in Touggourt so memorable. Even to this day, I am fully persuaded that God sent me to that desert town to be taught one of the greatest spiritual lessons I have ever learnt; a lesson that not only proved vital for the days I was there, but also for the years to come.

It came about in the following way. From the roof of my house, I could clearly observe the activities of the town's inhabitants. Day after day and several times a day, I noticed how all the men would immediately respond to the call to prayer made from the minarets of the mosques by the local iman. As the call to prayer was being made, all the men of the town would place their prayer mats down on dusty streets and kneel to pray to their god.

Being, to my knowledge, the only Christian in that community and surrounded by so many sincere people of a different faith, I felt compelled to seek God as to why I was so presumptuous to think that what I believed was right and everybody else in that town was possibly praying to the wrong god (or so I had been taught at Bible college).

At best, I only prayed twice a day and that in private, whilst around me everyone, without hesitation, would stop and pray publicly five times a day. Being just one amongst so many compelled me to inquire of God as to which religion, if any, was right!

To this end, I spent much time seeking God in prayer and reading my Bible. Eventually, with these issues burning deep within my heart, I believe the Holy Spirit led me to the book of Ephesians. There, in chapter one, I discovered the incredible provision God has made for sinners such as myself. I took special note of the amazing power of transformation promised to all who believe in Jesus. I read chapter one several times with great excitement and in particular, verses 13-14. Amazingly, I believe the Holy Spirit revealed the truth of these verses to me in a most remarkable and relevant way.

As I reread them again and again, I suddenly leapt to my feet with a heart bursting with great joy and excitement, for God had just answered my prayer. In exactly the way that Jesus had promised His disciples, the Holy Spirit illuminated my understanding with a revelation of truth.

God's Spirit clearly revealed to me that all who respond to the message of Jesus by faith, having repented and turned from their past sin and now believing the promises of God, would receive a "guarantee of authenticity" that Jesus is the only way to God and heaven. To the best of my knowledge, there is no other religion on earth that offers such a "guarantee of authenticity."

For me, this is a miracle of God's grace, as it is written in the Revised Standard Version, Ephesians 1:13-14, *"In him [Jesus] you also, who have heard the word of truth, the gospel of your salvation, and have believed in him, were sealed with the promised Holy Spirit, which is the guarantee of our inheritance until we acquire possession of it, to the praise of his glory."*

For the very first time in my life, I began to understand that the gift and ministry of the Holy Spirit in a believer's life, is God's guarantee that he or she will inherit eternal life. This makes Christianity the only religion on earth to offer a guarantee of authenticity.

There in the isolation of the Sahara Desert, the Holy Spirit assured me that God's promise of forgiveness, transformation, and eternal salvation is sealed with an unbreakable promise of God given to every believer. Therefore, at that moment, it was with great confidence that I believed that God, by the power of the Holy Spirit, had called me, changed me, and filled my understanding with the knowledge of eternal truth that was provided through the sacrifice of the Lord Jesus.

I could now declare, as the apostle Paul wrote in 2 Timothy 1:12 (NIV), *"I am not ashamed, because I know whom I have believed, and am convinced that he is able to guard what I have entrusted to him for that day."* At that moment, I knew I had made the right choice when I entrusted my life into the hands of God, who later was to take me through the valley of the shadow of death where I would need the assurance of the guaranteed presence of the Holy Spirit.

Did I dance with joy as God revealed this truth to me? I certainly did, for I was able to identify the incredible work of the Holy Spirit in the transformation of my own life. As a fellow student in Bible college once said to me, "If this is what you are like now, I'm glad I never met you before you were a Christian." How right he was, and how wonderful it is that God hasn't finished with me yet.

Since that time, the Holy Spirit has guaranteed day after day that I am a child of God regardless of my background. Those days spent in the little walled town of Touggourt will never be forgotten. Like Paul in the Bible, who also met with God in the desert, my time there proved to be a great place in which to get many things sorted with God, before attempting to share His gospel in dangerous places.

A few days after the encounter with God I was summoned back to Algiers by the mission director. The journey could be described as "interesting." It involved leaving Touggourt at around three in the afternoon by taking a desert taxi to Ouargla. The taxi driver would only leave when he had a full load of five passengers. Fortunately, on this occasion, there were five of us waiting to travel, along with all our luggage. It then took several hours of driving through vast stretches of straight and empty desert roads to reach our destination.

On the way, we passed an occasional oasis where I saw a camel or two, but otherwise, the desert is just sand for mile after mile after mile in every direction. Having reached Ouargla, I discovered that the bus to Algiers was not due to leave until four in the morning. This meant having to spend the night trying to sleep on an empty street. I can only say that a desert town is a very lonely place at two a.m., apart from cockroaches. Fortunately, the bus left on time.

The bus journey was of special interest to me for it was the first time I heard and understood colloquial Arabic. On this occasion, it was spoken by the bus driver who was being very rude to a local passenger he called "a silly old cow." Well, I had to start understanding the local language somewhere!

Eventually, I arrived safely back in Algiers. Once there, the mission leader explained that he had received a request from mission headquarters. My sister had asked if I could attend her forthcoming wedding. He reluctantly agreed and suggested that while there, I should enquire into the possibility of purchasing a Land Rover for my own use, which I would have to purchase from any funds I could raise for such an expensive vehicle.

With every expectation of returning to Algeria within just a few weeks, I boarded the aircraft for which I had been given a ticket, to attend the wedding in the UK.

Chapter 5
A Change of Direction

Following the celebration of my sister's wedding, a Christian butcher and his wife graciously offered me the use of a room above their butcher's shop located within a small shopping area. We were members of the same church and knew each other well, not just because of church connections, but because the couple were also good friends who understood the journey I had embarked upon.

Their generosity provided me with the opportunity to seek God's will concerning purchasing the vehicle I required for use in the desert, as prescribed by the mission director. This had now become a major issue for me. In the first place, I did not know how to raise the funds required, but equally challenging was the fact that I knew the running costs of the vehicle were far beyond anything I could expect to raise on a regular basis.

At that time, I had no money, no peace, and no desire to pursue the issue. I would have had to drive it from the UK across France, Spain, Gibraltar, Morocco, and into Algeria. It was clear to me that I was out of sync with God concerning the whole matter. As much as I would have found running around the desert in a suitable vehicle exciting, I knew I was lacking God's sign of approval on the whole idea.

A few days after accepting the use of the room, I had the opportunity to commit myself to a season of earnest prayer concerning all the issues before me. I had already made an appointment with a Christian car dealer, but before meeting him I needed to know God's will concerning this issue.

Although, as a novice Christian, I was reckless enough to take a so-called "step of blind faith" and proceed with the purchase; on this occasion, I felt compelled to seek God for a very clear Yes or No concerning the matter. Taking "blind steps of faith" is never a good practice, although I had taken some very significant steps of faith based upon the Word that God had revealed to me, such as the time I attended Bible college.

The time I set aside to pray concerning these issues was now vital to me. Midway through the day, whilst in an attitude of total dependence upon God and still waiting before Him for clarity and direction, I was suddenly surprised to hear the butcher running up the stairs, loudly calling my name.

"Phil! Phil!" he cried, as he burst into my room without knocking. In his excitement, he was disconcertingly waving his butcher's cleaver around in my direction.

Breathing heavily from the exertion of running up the stairs, he eventually managed to blurt out that God had just spoken to him. Apparently, this unexpected divine communication had happened whilst he was serving a customer a joint of meat down in his shop. He insisted that God wanted me to read Psalm 27 immediately. Having delivered his message, he returned to his shop, still clutching the cleaver. I have no idea what the unsuspecting customer thought, but I turned to my Bible to read the psalm anyway.

Despite my thoughts concerning the butcher's actions, I read the psalm he had mentioned several times and the fourteenth verse stood out to me*: "Wait patiently for the Lord. Be brave and courageous. Yes, wait patiently for the Lord"* Psalm 27:14 NLT.

I already knew that if I was to be useful to God in the desert, I needed to be out from under the field leader's feet, but was God indicating that for now, I should just wait? Although I did not understand why I accepted the verses of this psalm as God's word for me.

Subsequently, I telephoned the car dealer, whom I knew to be an honest man, and arranged to meet him later that day. Having met with him, I shared the psalm that the butcher had brought to my attention. We then chatted and prayed together concerning the whole issue of a vehicle and agreed that at this stage in my missionary career it would be beyond my means to purchase and maintain a vehicle in desert conditions. With Psalm 27 in our minds, we agreed it would be better to "wait patiently upon the Lord" until He revealed more of His will concerning my future.

Amazingly, within just a couple of weeks of deciding not to purchase a vehicle, the mission was ordered by the Algerian government to cease its activities in the desert, making my need for a vehicle immediately totally redundant. Consequently, a few weeks later, I resigned from the mission and began seeking God for redirection in my life.

The important lesson I learnt concerning this issue was the necessity of allowing God's peace to rule my heart in all my decision-making. By nature, I can be quite irrational and I found it all too easy to allow the urgency of the moment to dictate what I did or did not do.

Through this experience, God was teaching me the necessity of waiting patiently upon Him, not just for the need of the moment but also for an understanding of His timing concerning everything I was involved with, even matters of the heart.

I know God views my life from the perspective of having a perfect understanding of everything about me, everything that surrounds me, and everything about my future, whereas I find it difficult to see beyond my current need or crisis. It is only through spending time waiting upon God that I can receive clarity, provision, and protection for faith to act within the bigger picture of life surrounding me.

After I resigned from the mission, the following days proved to be very difficult for I now lacked direction in my decision-making. Although I accepted that it was not God's will for me to return to the Sahara (although I had never actually given any thought as to how long God would want me there), I really did not know what my next move should be.

During this time, I had to believe that my future was held safe in the hands of God and that according to His promise, He would direct my paths. Deep within the inner recesses of my heart, the only certainty I had was knowing that I was resolute about following Jesus for the rest of my life. Therefore, once again I needed to take time to seek His will concerning my life.

Following a season of prayer, little did I suspect that within a relatively short time I would be on my way to Sierra Leone for two years, with a commitment to be married immediately upon my return!

Fortunately, or divinely, a week after leaving the mission, I had the opportunity to attend a Bible conference in the south of England where I met a man going to Freetown. We had much in common and, although our backgrounds could not have been more different, his primary objective was street evangelism.

During the week of the conference, we enjoyed good fellowship and, when the week ended, I said to him, "Dave, I'm not sure what God wants me to do, but I'm willing to help you for a couple of years in Freetown if that suits you." With a positive response from Dave, it was agreed that I should join him in West Africa as soon as possible. With the gift of hindsight, I later wished I had researched where Sierra Leone was and what Freetown was like before making such a commitment.

It wasn't possible for me to leave the UK immediately as I needed to undertake an orientation course with the mission Dave served with. Also, I had promised to help at a Christian youth camp in Dundrum, Northern Ireland, as the sports officer for a month. At the camp, I was kept very busy with various duties. Behind the camp was a great view of the mountains of Mourne rising majestically and filling the horizon with their magnificence, whilst the camp itself looked out over the Irish Sea.

The padre, or Bible teacher of the camp for the month, was a young lady named Sylvia, who had recently graduated as a schoolteacher. Being interested in missions, she had just been accepted for missionary training at the Glasgow Bible College.

This was a two-year course that would commence very shortly after the closing of camp. As can happen on these occasions, we had the opportunity to spend time together and sometimes we talked about other things besides camp business. Following a day's busy schedule, we occasionally took a stroll together to view the wonders of God's creation and chat about a few other things we were curious about! Following the closing of the camp, we arranged to meet up in Belfast for a dinner date or two.

Sometime later, whilst she was attending Bible college, I had the opportunity to speak in churches around the Glasgow area. This provided us with a chance to meet up and on one occasion, we spent a wonderful day around Loch Lomond just walking and talking.

On this, the third occasion of our being together, we returned to Glasgow where I managed to pluck up the courage to say to her, "I'm off to Africa for two years and you will be attending Bible college over the same period. Will you marry me when I return?"

Amazingly, she said "Yes" and added, "But I'm not going to Africa as a missionary," to which I replied, "and I'm not asking you to." Around the same time, the leaders of a little chapel asked if I would construct a baptistery for them. I was glad to help and from the profit, purchased our engagement ring.

Most, if not all my friends understand the wisdom of the proverb, "Look before you leap." Unfortunately, I tend to leap before I look! The outcome is that I will normally go where I believe God is leading me before asking all the relevant questions. Despite the simplicity or naivety of my approach, God has never failed to provide for my every need, but I have experienced some challenging situations that I was unprepared for. Although God has always protected me from danger and often prevented me from making wrong decisions, I sometimes still get things wrong; but God has always been quick to pardon and forgive and redirect me.

Therefore, it seemed quite normal for me to agree to serve the Lord for two years in Sierra Leone before asking all the relevant questions, and on this occasion, it proved to be a great mistake. With the help of my church and income derived from construction work, I was able to raise the required funds for a flight and some of the other expenses that would be incurred, to begin the two-year Christian ministry in Freetown.

Apart from knowing that Sierra Leone was in West Africa, I knew almost nothing about the country. Regrettably, I was now a candidate for a big wake-up call and some big surprises.

Chapter 6
Life in Freetown

Just a few weeks following my engagement to Sylvia, I arrived at Lungi, Sierra Leone's international airport. It was around midday and, although I had endured the heat of the desert, I was quite unprepared for the humid conditions that immediately began to sap my energy. Even as I descended the steps of the aircraft, I was overwhelmed with heat and immediately regretted wearing a new woollen suit I had just purchased for the trip!

Sweating profusely, I was much relieved to find my new companion, Dave, among the milling crowds. He was dressed in a short-sleeved shirt, tropical shorts, long socks, and sturdy shoes. I think he smiled at my new suit before escorting me through the confusion of immigration and customs procedures, where all around me were people shouting and pushing in ways I had never experienced before.

I was now in a country where the British custom of queuing had been totally rejected and noticed that seasoned travellers were handing out "monetary gifts" to gain favoured attention from immigration and customs officers. Along with all the normal local African "palavers," or ways of speaking heatedly together that only seasoned travellers to these places understand, I eventually made it through passport control and customs before stepping out for the first time into the land of Sierra Leone with instructions to report to immigration headquarters in Freetown within three days.

Our journey from the airport into the city of Freetown, the country's capital, was bewildering. It was my first exposure to an unexpected onslaught of noise, colour, and smells. All around me were overflowing rickety market stalls, abandoned rubbish, and inquisitive children. Everywhere I turned, I was greeted by people with smiling faces, many of whom caught my attention by calling out, "White man, white man, hello, hello."

Within a few hours of landing at the airport, I gratefully arrived at what was to be my new home, a rented apartment in the centre of the downtown area of Freetown. The very first thing I did was to dress down into shorts and a T-shirt and drink glass after glass of filtered water.

Later that day, as we approached evening, since it was becoming just a little cooler whilst remaining very humid, my new friend Dave took me on my first walk through the city of Freetown. I was struck by the fact that every building had a watchman, and every vehicle was driven with its horn blaring. Scrawny dogs were everywhere and were scavenging through roadside rubbish tips or dumps, fighting, or just barking.

After an hour or so of walking, we eventually entered an area of the city known as King Tom. It was here that Dave had accepted an invitation to visit a small local church in an area which, many years previously, had been occupied by British naval personnel. Two very ancient cannons were still visible in what were once the grounds of British naval officers, but were now occupied by Baptist missionaries.

As evening turned to night, we eventually found the church we were looking for. By the time we arrived, it was already filling with Africans from the neighbourhood who were attending their regular evening meeting. Soon after we arrived, a drummer began to gently beat a rhythm to which the enthusiastic African congregation began to sway and shuffle. As the rhythm of the drum increased, locally made maracas accompanied it until suddenly the entire congregation burst out with their locally inspired songs and began a shuffling dance.

We, however, as westerners, in attempting to enter the spirit of the occasion, began stomping around like a couple of lost giraffes in a herd of gazelles.

It was on this, my first evening in a West Africa church, that I encountered mosquitoes that seemed to come at me like miniature aircraft. Whilst buzzing away above my head, they would dive bomb me, yet always remaining just beyond a swipe of my hands. After making their presence known, the sneaky little creatures would silently alight on any part of my flesh that was exposed in order to refuel themselves with my blood, whilst downloading their deadly malaria into my body.

Even more disturbing on this first tropical evening were the sausage flies. These four-inch sausage-shaped creatures, equipped with wings, would fly in zigzag patterns about three inches above the ground, seemingly having no idea where they were going. My first instinct was to dodge them, but as they never actually flew into me, I found it best to ignore their aimless flight, as I was trying my best to participate in this, my first visit to a West African church.

As the evening wore on and I continued to prance away, totally out of sync with the beat of the music, I was suddenly overwhelmed by everything happening around me. In just the flash of a moment, I had to sit down, for this had been one, if not the most extraordinary day of my life. I now felt a world away from the wonderful days of isolation in the Sahara Desert, and it was only twelve hours ago that I was saying goodbye to my fiancée in the modern western world.

But now, right at this moment, it seemed that God had chosen to immerse me into a baptism of culture amongst people of one of the most impoverished nations on earth, and it was all feeling just a bit too much for me.

To add to the culture shock, the pastor of the church walked over to me and unexpectedly invited me to address the congregation. Already overcome by the experience of being there, I was also overwhelmed at his invitation. Swamped with a mixture of privilege, bewilderment, responsibility, embarrassment, and perspiration, I could not refuse the pastor's request.

So, I stepped forward and up onto the platform where he, who knew absolutely nothing about me, introduced me to the congregation in glowing terms whilst bestowing many questionable tributes upon me.

Standing there, feeling very much out of place, I lifted my eyes to survey the congregation and immediately became transfixed. There, in the back row of the church, I noticed a huge African woman with gigantic breasts unashamedly satisfying the thirst of every child under the age of about ten years. I have to admit I found this sight somewhat of a distraction that caused me to lose even the few limited thoughts I had for this occasion.

Nevertheless, I managed to rise to the challenge of addressing the congregation by pretending I was accustomed to all I saw and heard. I steadfastly spoke with my slightly London cockney accent to this Creole-speaking congregation and stuck to the task of trying to inform them that Jesus is the Good Shepherd, and we, being His sheep, will always be led by Him if we choose to follow Him.

As it happened, the message was totally inappropriate, as the local and youthful African shepherds never lead their sheep, anyway. They normally guide their flocks, which are often mixed with similar-looking goats, by driving them with skilfully thrown rocks and stones. That evening, I think the congregation found me as curious as I found them, and after a very long day that had begun in London, that evening proved to be just a little too much for this Englishman's first foray into the tropics!

I was very grateful to return to our flat, have a cold shower, and crash out on my bed. It had been a long day, but the night was to be no better! No sooner had I settled onto, but never into bed, due to the very high humidity and heat, the local dance band struck up just across the road in the town hall with African rhythmic music at full volume. The dance continued until three in the morning, at which time I thought the sleep I longed for would bring refreshment. However, once the music ceased, the mosquitoes surrounding my protective net could now be heard. Emitting their high-pitched buzzing sound whilst attempting to get at me through the netting, they were now successfully disturbing my rest.

Also, the relative humidity was getting to me. It was giving me the feeling that I was trying to sleep in a sauna. Although I hadn't noticed it before, it seemed that every dog in Freetown was now joining in the chorus of this endless night. As I lay there on my bed, tossing, sleepless, and saturated with perspiration, I could hear a nearby domestic fight. Later I discovered that wife - or girlfriend-beating, accompanied by the inevitable cries of pain, was just part of a normal night's activity.

At this, the end of my first day and very long night in the tropics, I knew I was absolutely out of my depth.

Having recovered from these first encounters, Freetown proved to be a fascinating city and could be described as vibrant, colourful, noisy, welcoming, and always smiling. Yet behind the smiles, there lurked great pain and poverty. At that time, Christianity as a religion flourished, but the experience of a living relationship with God, in which He meets the needs of those who call upon Him, was sadly lacking. Christianity seemed to offer more of a community status than salvation from sin. The vital transformation of a repentant sinner leading to eternal life, through faith in God, appeared to be absent.

Therefore, over the following weeks, it was with some urgency that Dave and I walked the streets of the city. We visited hospitals, entered institutions that supposedly cared for the mentally deranged, held home Bible studies, and preached in every type of denominational church we came across, many of which we had never heard of before. We also assisted with the ministries of Scripture Union, Youth for Christ, and the Christian Literature Crusade. In doing so, I had never been happier or busier in my life.

From the veranda of our flat on Water Street, I could overlook the ancient Freetown harbour and jetty where, two hundred years previously, sailing ships docked with returning, liberated, or unwanted slaves from Western countries. In those days, as the slaves disembarked from the ships alongside the waterside jetty, they ascended the "King's Steps" until reaching the King's Gate, which remains there to this day.

As the slaves passed through the King's Gate, they officially stepped out of slavery and into freedom. Just a few hundred yards away, in the centre of the town, stood a giant cotton tree where liberated slaves would join in songs of praise, giving thanks to God for their freedom. This part of the world, still known as "White Man's Grave," seems to ignore the fact that hundreds, if not thousands, of returning slaves also lost their lives on what was once known as the "Mosquito Coast." After celebrating their "day of freedom," life expectancy for the liberated slaves was often very short!

Also, from our balcony, I could look out across the Atlantic Ocean towards the horizon. Dotted all around were heavy handmade dugout canoes, which brave and skilful fishermen used in their employment. Various forms of fishing techniques were used. Some would deploy great lengths of netting in a circular pattern and haul away for ages, dragging the heavy netting back on board. Others, in lighter craft, would skilfully stand in the centre of their dugouts and cast circular weighted nets into the sea from above their heads.

Unfortunately, there were also a few fishermen who would illegally throw a stick or two of dynamite over the sides of their boats and, following the explosion, pick up the resulting mess. Thankfully, that practice was brought to an end by the government. Whatever fishing techniques were employed, there was always an abundant choice of fish to be had in the local market, ranging from barracuda to local sardines. Combined with an abundance of tropical fruit, we never went hungry.

Water Street, on which our flat was located, is extremely broad at the point of our rented apartment. This was to accommodate railway lines or tracks that ran down the centre of the street and were narrower than the British railway lines. Freetown City Station was located just a hundred yards to our right and sometimes the little engines would steam right through the station and pass in front of our apartment. Having changed tracks, the engines would be coupled to their carriages for the up-line return journey into the interior regions of Sierra Leone. It was always a glorious sight to see these little engines chuffing up and back on that short stretch of road under a full head of steam and smoke.

Primarily, the rail system had been constructed for the diamond industry, it being deemed the safest way to transport diamonds through the jungle on the two-hundred-mile trip from the mines to the relative safety of the city offices.

After the first year in Freetown, my church in the UK sent money to purchase a small motorbike. Oh, what bliss!

Freetown is built in a horseshoe shape around the famous Mount Aureol, the principal mountain in the Lion Mountain range. From that day on, I no longer had to walk everywhere. I could now take great joy in escaping the humidity of the city by riding up into the relative coolness of the mountains. Although throughout the two years I was in Freetown, I lived in relative poverty; I lacked for nothing. God, in His grace, supplied my every need through the love and support of friends, both in the UK and the Christian expatriate community living in Freetown.

One of the many blessings of my adopted lifestyle was the privilege of being exposed to the lives of the indigenous people where I was able to relate to street traders, local boys and girls, the poorer families, and above all, the Créole people. Being accepted as "the white man," as I was called by so many, gave me a great opportunity to forge many friendships. I was often invited to address various established churches, mission churches, and in particular, indigenous churches; many of which had strange and questionable customs.

By God's grace, I was able to relate to and encourage several church leaders during that time. There is a saying in Freetown that contains a lot of truth: "It's not what you know that matters but who you know." Knowing so many of the good and great citizens of that city paved the way for me to help many of them when the horrendous civil war broke out ten years later. In many ways, Freetown has been very "Christianised" with every form of Christian denomination imaginable.

Most of my Freetown friends would identify as being born again, Bible-believing demonstrative Christians, who live alongside a plethora of churches with some very strange practices. One of the little congregations I sometimes visited during the week held a daily service after the sun had set at around 7 p.m. The service would gradually drift towards full participation as the musicians began beating their drums and the women enthusiastically shook their maracas.

As the feet of the congregation began shuffling, a lead voice would break out in song and the congregation would begin to repeat or respond to the lead singer. As the evening wore on, the tempo of the dancing increased until all who gathered were perspiring freely. As is common in these churches, there is often a white bucket of holy water that is kept beside the altar of the church. At an appropriate moment, the pastor or priest in charge of the service would slowly walk down the central isle of the church and with the use of a thick sprig of hyssop, sprinkle or shower the dancing congregation with water from the holy white bucket to cool them down. This was also the moment when the pastor invited me to address the congregation.

I never allowed my approval or disapproval of the customs and practices of churches, whether traditional or indigenous, to hinder an opportunity to share the Word of God. On one occasion, following my teaching session, the prophet of the church stood up and stated that as I was speaking, he saw me floating three feet in the air. Having assured him that I was not and that both my feet were firmly on the ground, I left the congregation broken-hearted, for I was banned from speaking there again after challenging the prophet. The Bible identifies such people as blind leaders of the blind who, in my opinion, not only rob the congregation of the truth of Jesus but also lead them in the ways of error and fear.

Walking through the centre of Freetown one evening, I came across an open-air meeting and stopped to listen. The prophet who spoke was dressed in black from head to toe, which should have alerted me, but as I was only visiting the city on this occasion, I waited to see what would happen. At the close of the meeting, the prophet in black came over to me and insisted that he should pray for me. Mostly due to the fact that the city was on war alert, I reluctantly consented. As he prayed over me, I was overcome with a heaviness of heart and a sense of alienation from God.

Although I immediately knew that I had done wrong, I was unable to shake the heaviness until I confessed my stupidity to my African brother, Richard. How I thank God that the heaviness lifted when Richard prayed, but I learnt a serious lesson; I should never allow or surrender to the prayer of another unless I am willing to accept the spirit that is within him or her. How I thank God for the Scripture where it is written that "The Lord is the Spirit, and wherever the Spirit of the Lord is there is freedom" 2 Corinthians 3:17 NLT. Following my brother's prayer, my freedom in God was restored.

The following day, I fell into conversation with one of the sad-looking prostitutes loitering around the hotel. We chatted for an exceedingly long time as she told me her story. She had fallen in love with a Dutchman and from that relationship, a daughter had been born, but the Dutchman had returned to Holland. Every day she expected his return, but until he did, the only way she could get the money she needed to live was through prostitution.

That day, I told her about Jesus and His love. I shared that He was willing to become the substitutional sacrifice for all our sin. Having understood what I was saying, she turned to God in repentance for salvation and acceptance of eternal life with Christ.

The following day, my friend and I visited her at her house for the purpose of giving her a Bible and sharing more of the story of God's love. We were somewhat surprised to discover that her house wasn't a shack, but rather a small, well-built building that was immaculately clean and tidy. Her little girl was bright and cheerful and doing well at school. After reading her the Scriptures, we handed her the Bible, for which she was very grateful. I do not know if she abandoned her immoral trade, but yet again, I caught just a glimpse of the pain, the indignity, the suffering, and the desperation of people who have to strive and beg for the basic necessities of life. As I prayed for her that day, I realised that only a great, wonderful, holy, and compassionate God can help such people.

Chapter 7
Belfast, Bullets, and Marriage

My two-year commitment to street evangelism in Freetown passed all too quickly. Apart from being hospitalised with a bout of malaria during which I thought my end had come, my time in Sierra Leone was brilliant. I had toured the country with the Christian Literature Crusade bookmobile distributing Bibles and Christian books, been involved with the Youth for Christ movement, along with Scripture Union events, and had the privilege of leading many home Bible study groups. Unfortunately, towards the end of my two-year commitment, my funding and support from the UK was minimal, which tended to make life very difficult at times.

During my two years in West Africa, I learnt many vital cross-cultural lessons, including the importance of family life in an African society, the value of friendship, and maybe above all, that I could trust my African friends with my life, something that actually happened on more than one occasion.

But now, my time in West Africa was coming to an end and with the help of my family, friends, and church back in the UK, I managed to purchase an air ticket for the return flight to the UK. Preparation for leaving was very simple as I only possessed what I stood up in, consisting of a pair of trousers, a shirt with a torn sleeve, a pair of well-worn shoes and socks, along with my Bible. All I now needed to leave the country was an exit visa and a small bag for carrying gifts for my family, especially my fiancée. Two years of walking the streets of the city had left me well bronzed by the tropical sun and very fit.

What a contrast London was to Freetown the morning I arrived back at Heathrow from where I would go to my parents' home for a few days. Although it was mid-June in 1971, it was also what some people would identify as a typical British summer's day as it was cold, grey, and drizzly. Jackets, raincoats, and umbrellas, along with the mandatory briefcase, were all part of the essential dress for most other travellers. I possessed none of these items, so with my shirt sleeves rolled up, I tried to stroll nonchalantly through customs and immigration without shivering. But without the suitable clothing, it was difficult.

The excitement of seeing my fiancée for the first time in two years helped me to embrace the re-entry procedures back into Britain. With nothing to declare, I quickly made my way through immigration and customs and suddenly began to feel out of place. As I approached the doors of the arrival hall, I became nervous and felt quite vulnerable.

The legacy of having lived in the tropics for two years suddenly overwhelmed me and I was forced to stop for a moment to prepare myself for what lay ahead. I realised it wasn't just that I was about to pass through the airport doors and back into the UK. It was far more than that. I knew that at this moment I was about to step out of my adopted African lifestyle and back into the Western world.

For a brief moment, these two worlds felt a million miles apart. Just eight hours previously, I had been fully embedded in African ways and surrounded by many friends. Now I was about to step back into the land of my birth, not knowing what the future held, apart from marriage.

I paused a few moments longer, took a deep breath, and deliberately stepped through the re-entry doors and into my future, having braced myself for whatever lay ahead. As the automatic doors slid back, I scanned the faces of all the expectant people waiting for loved ones, friends, or visitors.

Then I saw her; she was there, standing a little apart from the crowd. She was waiting just for me—it was Sylvia. We spotted each other simultaneously and with eyes only for each other, we met and shyly shared a hug, our first in two years. What a moment! As we stood together, I began to shiver. Maybe it was the cold or maybe it was the circumstances, but happily, my wife-to-be had brought a gift for me. It was a white Aran jumper that she had been knitting over the past months, ensuring its readiness for my return. I slipped it on immediately and, for several weeks, hardly took it off. What a gift, what a girl! Of course, we got married!

The return to the UK closed a big chapter in my life. Within a few weeks, I would no longer be a carefree single. Sylvia and I planned to be married within three months of my arrival and we set the date for Saturday, September 9, 1971. This meant I now had many things to attend to, like raising money for the wedding, moving to Northern Ireland, finding work, adjusting to a new lifestyle, and having to agree on any future missionary decisions with my wife-to-be.

As I look back over my years as a single person, I remain amazed at the faithfulness of God, even to this day. It was God who led me to a Bible college, into the Sahara Desert, then on to Freetown, and now to Belfast, in Northern Ireland.

I knew it was God's will that we should marry because He had told me so! To which Sylvia added, "I also hope it's because you love me." I have to acknowledge that I married her for both reasons. You may wonder how God "told" me that Sylvia was the one I should marry and, as unconventional as it may be for those who live in the West, I'll tell you.

Even when I met Sylvia at camp in Northern Ireland, I knew I would be going to Africa. Sylvia, on the other hand, had her sights set on being a missionary in Eastern Europe. I realised that these two visions were incompatible, so with some reluctance, before going to West Africa for the first time, I sat down to write a letter to her, terminating our romantic journey. As I put pen to paper, God spoke into the deep recesses of my heart through His Holy Spirit, asking, "What are you doing?" It was not an audible voice, but a clear and distinguishable inner voice of conviction that only the Holy Spirit can bring to bear upon a child of God.

So real was that moment that I replied audibly by saying, "I'm terminating my relationship with Sylvia."

The inner conviction of God simply said, "Don't do that." So, I tore the letter up.

Now that I was back in the UK, plans for the wedding became our priority and once again I, (soon to become we), experienced the fact that where God leads, God supplies. With every step of obedience we have taken, our faithful God has always supplied our every need.

Within hours of arriving back in the UK, I was asked if I would assist with the building of a substantial church extension. It was a huge challenge, which took many hours of hard work, but it was also God's provision. In partnership with a local builder and under the watchful eye of a Christian architect, we set to work, determined to have the extension to the church finished before my wedding.

Having completed the building work, I then moved to Belfast where Sylvia was living, so that together we could prepare for our wedding.

Almost immediately Sylvia and I were offered a flat owned by a Christian house agent, which we accepted and into which I was able to move immediately.

We were married on September 9, 1971, in Finaghy, just south of Belfast in Sylvia's home church. It was a very traditional wedding, enlivened by the arrival of an army helicopter full of British combat troops. Having landed just across the road from the church, fully armed troops immediately discharged from it and spread out, presumably seeking members of terrorist groups. Our wedding guests were very distracted from our wedding proceedings by the activities of the army.

Following the reception, and in our haste to get away to catch the evening ferry to Scotland for our honeymoon, I forgot our passports, and we subsequently missed the ferry. Having to wait for the next ferry, we arrived so late that we lost our booking at the hotel.

But we eventually reached Tenby in South Wales and began the journey of married life together. Following our honeymoon, we returned to Belfast and moved into our top-floor flat where most nights, we would go to bed to the sound of bullets whining down the Antrim Road as the British Army engaged with members of the IRA in running gun battles, accompanied by the regular explosions of detonating bombs. Sometimes it seemed like I was back in West Africa during one of the many coup attempts I experienced, but the situation in Belfast was far more serious and deadly.

Just two weeks into married life, Sylvia and I decided to have a midday lunch in a local restaurant from which I had a violent allergic reaction to the shellfish I had eaten. About an hour after our lunch, we were shopping in a grocery store and I could feel my body worsening rapidly.

"I need a doctor," I said to my new wife, who had more important things on her mind, like shopping.

"I don't know one," came the reply from behind a stack of tins!

I continued to deteriorate. "Sylvia," I persisted, "I'm going to hospital right now, with or without you," and I staggered towards the door.

Sylvia joined me and we scrambled into our brightly painted orange and black car. I headed immediately for the nearest hospital, on the notorious Falls Road, which was a "no-go" area for most Protestants.

By the time we arrived, I was having to hold one eye open with my hand in order to see the road, whilst steering the car with the other hand. Arriving outside the hospital, I abandoned the car in the middle of the road and ran to the reception desk. Without looking up, a receptionist said, "Yes?"

I replied, as I now had to use both hands to keep both eyes open, "There's something wrong with me."

"Oh," she said, "you'd better lie down."

So I did, right there on the floor of the reception hall, for I was feeling pretty rough by this time. Thankfully, somebody came, picked me up, placed me on a trolley, and rushed me into a small consulting room where everything became a bit hazy.

I remember members of the medical team firing a barrage of crazy questions at me while I struggled with a sinking feeling inside my head. I could sense my heart thumping and it seemed to me that it was slowing down.

Thinking this was a good time to say a prayer, I prayed the simplest of all prayers, even as my mind was drifting. I clearly remember saying, "Look out, heaven; here I come, ready or not."

At that moment, someone stuck a needle into me, and I immediately knew I was going to recover. Whether heaven was expecting me or not, I'm not sure, but I did spend the approaching night in hospital, where I enjoyed an evening meal of tender chicken.

The next morning, several nurses filed into my room, obviously on a mission.

One of them was clearly agitated, and she looked me straight in the eye. Suddenly she burst out, "You're not a Christian."

I replied, "I never said I was. Why?"

"You're far too practical," she continued, to which I made no response.

It was then I noticed that one of the other nurses was an ex-student from Emmanuel, the Bible college I had attended. She must have informed the agitated nurse of my Christian faith. But I liked the nurse's outburst and took it as a compliment, for I prefer to demonstrate my faith in God rather than just preach at people.

For me, being a Christian is not all about being religious; rather, it has everything to do with being related; that is, being related to God. My relationship with God began all those years ago in Gravesend when, having been convicted of my many sins by the power of the Holy Spirit, I confessed those sins to God, who forgave each and every one of them. That was the moment when, as the Bible puts it, I was born again by the power of God and I became a child of God.

God had just granted me a new beginning, and a guaranteed place in heaven. As the old song goes, "I don't know why Jesus loved me, but I'm glad that He does." All I know is that God chose me to be one of His witnesses, and my response to Him was "Yes."

Right there, as I lay in that hospital room, I knew my relationship with God was secure and that death held no fear over me. I was ready to meet my God and the prayer I had made earlier in the hospital was not trivial. I just wanted to ensure that heaven was ready for me! I recovered rapidly from the reaction and knew that God was not finished with me yet.

For the first few months of marriage, Sylvia and I saw very little of each other. She taught at a secondary school during the day, while I, having secured employment as a temporary prison officer, was placed on duty over many nights and most weekends.

My employment offered me a unique crash course for an Englishman requiring introduction into Irish culture. Whilst in Belfast, I took seriously the several life-threatening experiences I encountered and realised that my life was always and totally in the hands of God.

On our first Christmas Eve, whilst shopping for my wife's Christmas present, I had just moved away from the window of a downtown store in which was hidden an explosive device. As I moved away, the device exploded with an ear-shattering noise. With the shop's window and the display scattered all over the road, I knew I had missed death by seconds. This was not the only time my life had been spared!

Did I learn anything from these near-death experiences? I most definitely did. The God who called me is the God who protects me. He had promised to care for me and guide me through all of life's challenges. The events experienced in Belfast proved to be just a precursor for all that was to be encountered throughout our time in West Africa where, along with my family, we would be confronted by snakes and robbers, tropical diseases, African civil war, dangers seen and unseen, whilst all the time being protected by the grace and power of God who never failed us.

Both Sylvia and I knew we were called by God to be involved in some form of full-time Christian missionary activity even before we were married. Sylvia, having categorically stated that she would never go to Africa, was thinking God would send us to some place in Europe where she already knew a smattering of languages.

I happened to be more relaxed as to where or when God would eventually send us. One day Sylvia announced, with her great Irish resolve, which does not permit any contradiction or challenge from me, that she had asked God to show us where we were to go as missionaries and that He should do it before the year ended.

I thought that was just a little presumptuous of her as it was already December, but according to her faith, so be it!

Our little apartment, being on the third story of a converted house, was only accessible by an external steel stairway. We had reason to think that the people on the ground floor were sympathetic to the IRA movement and that the people living below us were not of a Protestant persuasion.

As a result of our observations, we made what we thought was an emergency plan, providing me with an escape from the house in the event of trouble due to my occupation and nationality. Our idea was that I would jump out of the top-floor window into a nearby tree. From there, I would climb down the tree and onto the road below. I never consented to a trial run or a rehearsal of this escape route, so will never know if it would have worked! Fortunately, the postman, who had to ascend the three flights of iron steps to deliver our mail, could descend the same way he came up.

On the very last day of the year, the date set by Sylvia for God to answer her prayer, we lay in bed listening to the postman as he clanged his way up the three-story iron stairway. Having reached our apartment, he pushed just one letter through the letterbox and it fell onto the doormat.

Sylvia, now full of expectation, went to collect it, believing it to be God's response to her prayer. She was, of course, quite right. It was God's response, and it came in the form of an airmail letter from missionaries in Sierra Leone. They had written to ask us if we would be willing to go to Freetown for a year, enabling them to take a furlough back in the UK. Amazingly, God had answered Sylvia's prayer on the very day she had stipulated. Without making any comment to me, we both said, "Yes" to God, for we knew that we would be accepting the invitation. So, she made breakfast!

After nine months of marriage, we welcomed our first child into our world. Christine was born in a hospital in downtown Belfast to the clatter of local gunfire, which prevented the doctor from attending the birth. Only a few bombs were detonated that day, but the one that was placed in a local hotel caused the closure of the main road leading to the hospital, which prevented me from being present at her birth. I don't think I would have been allowed to be present anyway, for such were the hospital regulations of the day.

An hour or two after our daughter was born, the roads having now been cleared of all the rubble caused by the bombs; I drove into Belfast to see my wife and for the very first time, my baby daughter. What a flood of emotions flowed through me as I ascended the hospital stairs to see our baby! I can still feel the tingle of tension, along with the excitement of seeing her.

Arriving at the ward, I found Sylvia sitting up in bed, glowing like a lamp and bursting with pride. She indicated a cot under the window. I approached it very carefully, and there, wrapped in a hospital blanket, was our tiny baby girl boasting a head of fine black hair. I moved the cot towards the window to get a better look at her but was immediately reprimanded by a nurse, who then officially introduced me to my baby.

The next few weeks became a whirl of visiting family, speaking at meetings, and packing suitcases for Freetown. I was amazed by how much I needed to take to Africa now that I had a wife and a baby daughter. No longer did just one simple cabin bag suffice! The date for our travel had been set, and we were booked to sail to Africa in just a few days' time, with Christine being just six weeks old.

The Friday before we left Belfast became known as Black Friday. Earlier that morning, Sylvia had gone to see her mother, who lived on the other side of town, and during that afternoon, thirteen bombs were detonated on the streets of Belfast city. Many key buildings were destroyed, including the rail station, the bus station, hotels, and petrol stations, all of which had been turned into heaps of rubble that were now blocking many roads. Telephone lines were down, and there was no other means of communication. At that moment, I did not know whether Sylvia and the baby were safe, or even where they were.

Having finished work for the day, I jumped into our old car and began navigating my way across the city. I needed to skirt great piles of rubble that, just an hour earlier, had been some of the city's greatest buildings.

Arriving at Grandma's house, it was an immense relief to find both mother and child safe. With hindsight, I can now see how God was using these acts of violence, in which many lives were lost, along with the mass destruction to major institutions and property, to display His protective love and power on those He had chosen to do His will.

We left Belfast a few days later, having experienced the worst of the conflict, and within five weeks we boarded the passenger ship *SS Aureol*, bound for Freetown.

Our ship sailed from Southampton, as had scores of missionaries centuries before, who, like us, knew they were called of God to serve Him in an area of the world known as White Man's Grave. Likewise, as we followed in their footsteps, we also stood at the rail of our ship and with our daughter in our arms waved a final farewell to our parents, who were now grandparents, standing on the dockside. They were waving their handkerchiefs with tears in their eyes, whilst there were great lumps in our throats. Together, our little family slowly sailed away from everyone and everything we knew and into an unknown future.

Since then, Sylvia and I have stood together through many monumental challenges; a few dangers, and several seasons of hardships. We have experienced rejection, heartbreak, inconvenience, challenging parenthood responsibilities, unexpected hosting of international visitors, tropical diseases and disappointments, all of which have been part of God's calling on our lives.

On the other hand, we have experienced times of great joy, happiness and fulfilment. We have lacked no good thing and have always been protected in times of danger. Above all, we know that we were always safe in the knowledge of God's will, having proved again and again that being in the will of God is the safest place on earth.

Before sailing to Freetown, as potential missionaries, we travelled around Northern Ireland speaking at various missionary meetings on deputation, seeking to raise money for our support, which we were not very successful at doing! Some of the places where the meetings were held were in strange locations, including what was originally a genuine chicken house from which the former feathered inhabitants had been evicted.

We had great difficulty finding this "place of worship," for it was still in the same field as other chicken houses that were occupied by chickens. It was only when a few top-of-the-range motor vehicles began arriving at the gate to the field that we realised we were in the right place. The little congregation that night was attentive to our tales of our missionary adventures, and very generous to our missionary cause, making it clear that the congregation was more willing to give to mission causes than to a so-called proper building.

Another remarkable supporter of missions we were privileged to spend time with was the proprietor of a typical Irish fish and chip shop. The shop was in an area of Belfast that had experienced much violence throughout the so-called Northern Ireland Troubles, accompanied by many bombs and bullets. It was a very busy and successful enterprise where this courageous man of God expressed his faith in God to all throughout the neighbourhood.

Every week, it was his practice to give the entire takings of a day's business to missions. At the close of sales on Thursday evenings, he placed all of the day's takings in a brown paper bag and gave it randomly to any missionary he met that day or the next. It was also his practice never to count the money that was in the till that day. My wife and I were greatly blessed to be among the recipients of such a strange act of generosity.

Chapter 8

A Family in West Africa

Our final days in Belfast had been hectic, challenging, and even dangerous, and now we were looking forward to a time of relaxation on our voyage to West Africa. Having travelled to England to say our goodbyes to other members of our family, we were taken by car to the Southampton port from where our ship would sail.

Several family members had come to see our departure, which enabled us to take a last opportunity to gather with them for prayer.

Having said our farewells and boarded the ship, we stood at the ship's railing, looking down on them with our baby in our arms. The ship's lines were eventually cast, allowing the ship to slowly move away from her moorings. Within our party, there was not a dry eye as we waved our handkerchiefs until our family members were out of view.

Our ten days on board the *Aureol* proved to be everything we needed. Throughout that time, we enjoyed good food, the company of good friends who unexpectedly were on the same ship, and quality family time, which included pushing our baby in her pram ten times around the deck to walk a mile.

Amazingly, having trusted friends to travel with greatly enhanced our sailing experience.

The ship docked for a short time in the Canary Islands, but all too soon, we began to draw close to West Africa.

Our first glimpse of Sierra Leone was of the Lion Mountains rising above the horizon. There are no lions there today, but a few leopards remain in the dense jungle, along with an abundance of exotic birds, butterflies, and six-meter-long snakes.

Drawing closer to land, we could begin to identify some of the buildings scattered around the base of Mount Aureol. Among the passengers, excitement was rising as now we could see other ships moored alongside the dock.

At this point, preparation for disembarking became the objective of every passenger. Along with many others, we packed and repacked our cases at least six times as we needed reassurance that our every possession was in them.

Finally, our bright red pram, in which our baby Christine took pride of place, was made ready for the arrival process. We knew from previous experiences that we could not afford to forget anything, especially documentation vital for every international traveller.

Eventually, the ship docked and was securely tied up at its berth, but it seemed to take forever as we waited in an endless queue before being allowed to approach the disembarkation control. Passports, health certificates, visas, luggage, pram, and baby were all made ready for inspection, but there was no movement among those waiting to disembark.

The longer we waited, the higher the temperature rose. The higher the temperature, the greater our awareness of the humidity. The greater the humidity, the shorter our patience became, and soon, grumbling among disembarking passengers was rising.

Suddenly, as though triggered by a starter's gun, a hoard of immigration officers descended on the ship, surrounded by the so-called porters. The porters clamoured around, shouting and poking us as they sought to "tote" our luggage on their heads for a price. Dock workers now appeared and began milling around the dockside, doing whatever only dockworkers seem to know what to do.

Uniformed police appeared and stood alongside the doors and passageways, looking either important or lost. Officials without uniforms began sullenly issuing commands and giving directions to anyone who would listen. Eventually, the immense queue of disembarking passengers began to move, but it only crawled very slowly in what we hoped was a forward direction towards the gangplanks and customs sheds.

Having descended from the ship, we sweated our way through a multitude of landing procedures, including being searched, along with all our luggage. We were examined, questioned, and eventually, our passports stamped. Finally, we emerged from the immigration sheds, feeling a little jaded and also confused, only to discover that the humid tropical air was no fresher outside the sheds than it had been inside.

The tropical heat and humidity of the day were causing us to perspire as never before, and the enthusiasm for the adventure we had embarked upon earlier that day was rapidly waning. Fortunately, just as we were being overwhelmed with the humidity and feelings of regret concerning the chaotic confusion around us, we spied a friendly face. The missionary, whom we were replacing for the year, had arrived to meet and greet us, and he was ready to transport us to our new home.

Having loaded us and all of our luggage and belongings into his small car, he drove us through the noisy, crowded, and colourful streets of

Freetown and into the Murraytown area of the city. We turned from the main highway onto a potholed track named Pipeline, where the city's water pipeline is fully visible.

Ascending a very steep incline, we passed through security gates and into the mission compound and parked on a concrete apron. At last, we had made it—we were home!

Our new home was a first-floor apartment in a large, fairly modern building containing a spacious living room, complete with a ceiling fan. It was airy and relatively cool, with large panoramic windows offering views across the river, where in the far distance we could see the international airport. Besides a kitchen and living room, the house comprised three bedrooms, a bathroom, and a balcony. It was all very luxurious, and it didn't take long before we started to relax within our new surroundings whilst the stress of the past few hours began to evaporate.

Immediately beyond our gated compound exists an impoverished community living in overcrowded stick and mud-dubbed huts often roofed with rusty and leaky corrugated pan roofs. Every Saturday, a local butcher would lead a cow, that had walked many miles, into the centre of the village to be hung in the butcher's favourite tree. The poor creature would hang there until most of it had been sold to waiting customers. Only when the butcher considered that he had received sufficient returns on his investment would he dispatch the beast, at which point every customer could claim the joint they had chosen and paid for.

By this time, local vultures, which had descended on the roof of our house, were waiting for the opportunity to fight over the scraps of the carcass that no one claimed or wanted. Purchasing the weekly joint was just one of the many tasks that Sylvia needed to attend to every Saturday morning.

The missionaries we were relieving left for the UK just a few weeks after our arrival. As I had already lived in Freetown for a couple of years, being on our own was not such a great challenge as we knew that this was the place where God had led us, and where He wanted us to be. Despite the challenge of adjusting to the humidity, culture, and African lifestyle, we were at peace within ourselves with the Holy Spirit witnessing to us that we were in the right place at the right time.

After we settled into an African lifestyle, hectic days followed in which there was never a dull moment! Sylvia was always busy with our baby and the many missionaries or visitors who would stay with us, often unannounced, whilst I worked in the bookshop that was always busy with customers. Having an air-conditioned reading room was popular with missionaries. Many came just to rest awhile in the cool during their shopping trips. The bookshop was in an area surrounded by street traders, some of whom had permission to lock their wares safely in the shop overnight. In return, they helped to protect us from thieves and robbers. They also kept us informed of potential problems, particularly of a political nature.

Driving in and around the overcrowded and chaotic streets of Freetown was always a challenge. Being the new white face in town, I was easily identified by the non-driving traffic police, who were on the lookout for someone to arrest for minor or imaginary driving infringements. Bribery and extortion supplemented their wages (if they were paid at all), and were accepted as part of their regular income.

Sometimes, when I passed a policeman who was on point duty directing traffic, he would jump down off his box, conscript a taxi, and pursue me concerning an imaginary driving infringement. When I noticed him doing this, I would drive around the block and back to the point of the supposed offence. This often resulted in the pursuing police officer being confused as to what my offence had now become. The original charge of failing to stop was now inappropriate, as I had now technically stopped. Nevertheless, I would be ordered to drive the policeman to traffic police headquarters on the other side of town, where I would be interviewed for several hours.

When I still refused to pay an acceptable sum of money for my unidentified "offence," normally a senior police officer came to my defence. I was once charged for having a moving wheel as I passed a policeman! I think the policeman was suggesting that the wheel wobbled as the car moved.

During those days, I came to understand the difference between bribery and extortion and for me there is an important distinction, especially as I did not want to be found guilty of bribery before God. My understanding is that a bribe is something offered by an offender as a legal obligation or to obtain an unmerited favour. I understand extortion as an excessive payment demanded by a person of power for their own profit. Understanding this has kept my heart at peace with God for many years, for I have been forced to pay extortionate sums many times and sometimes at gunpoint!

Does God have a sense of humour? Certainly, the Bible informs us that God laughs. Why should God choose someone who was compelled to leave school at fourteen and never voluntarily read a book until age eighteen, to be involved in Christian literature distribution? I cannot answer that question, but I can unequivocally state that I really enjoyed the challenge.

Despite my mistakes and obvious weaknesses, God blessed the ministry He had entrusted to me. Being accepted as the bookman and as someone without a doctrinal axe to grind, I was invited to speak in numerous churches throughout the city. Sylvia was also busily involved with correspondence courses, leading Bible study groups, holding children's meetings, and offering great hospitality to the many visitors who stayed in our home.

Sylvia, a qualified schoolteacher, held a Christian Sunday school session every week at the Milton School for blind children. Amazingly, every time we arrived at the school compound, the children came running to the gate, shouting "Hello, Mr Philip," as I was usually called.

One day, I asked them how they always knew I had entered their compound. The honest reply was, "No one else walks like you, Mr Philip." Ah, well, I only asked!

One afternoon at the Sunday school, Sylvia told the story of the blind man Jesus healed on the Sabbath day. The lesson having finished, a little boy raised his hand and asked, "Please, Miss, can Jesus heal me today?"

In my mind, I can hear the standard response Christians give, sometimes without regard or sensitivity to the situation in which the question has been asked. To say "Yes" without due thought or consideration is, in my opinion, disrespectful to the inquirer. Of course, Jesus can heal people today, but the inquirer had raised this question to another level. The question the little blind boy wanted an answer to was not whether Jesus could heal him, for we all believe that is possible. The question was, would Jesus heal him, that day at that time?

As I was to discover a few years later when horrendous atrocities were being committed against humanity by members of the teenage rebel army, including mass amputations of hands, arms, legs, and breasts, I can only give what God has given me to give, and say what God has given me to say. I must never promise to give that which is not mine to give, but I can pray with compassion, and I do, and sometimes with tears.

No matter how much my heart bleeds for the sufferer, my task is to introduce him or her to Jesus, who alone is the miracle worker. I should never attempt to perform God's miracles by myself. Yet I remain truly amazed at how many contemporary miracles I have witnessed. The first and maybe the greatest was the amazing transformation God accomplished in my own life. It was Jesus who rescued me from a disastrous failure and led me into the amazing experiences of being a missionary (I understand a missionary as someone sent by Jesus to accomplish a specific task).

As our time in West Africa drew to a close, Sylvia preceded me to the UK for the birth of our second child. A few weeks later, I received a telegram from her informing me that our second daughter, Amanda Jayne, had been born in Belfast to the theme tune of "The Archers," which was being broadcast on the hospital radio. Amanda was a very vocal baby and ensured that all within earshot knew she had arrived.

As soon as possible, and with mounting excitement, I booked a flight back to the UK to join the family, who were staying with their grandmother in Belfast. It was late in the evening when I arrived at Sylvia's mother's house, by which time both my daughters were asleep in their beds.

After greeting the household, I naturally wanted to see my new-born baby daughter for the very first time, so I headed for her bedroom. Having been warned by her mother not to waken her due to her very hearty and persistent cries, I opened the bedroom door and looked at her for the very first time. She was sleeping so peacefully.

Totally ignoring the warning I had been given; I lifted her with great care and held her closely with tears of joy filling my eyes. Then, lifting my other daughter, I gently held them both together. True enough, having now woken both children, I noticed that my new daughter did have a fine set of lungs, but her cries were music to my ears. There are times, especially during family separation, when being a missionary is very, very painful.

Chapter 9

Pushed to the Breaking Point

Over the years, I have been given opportunities to assist with the orientation of volunteers preparing for short-term mission adventures. On such occasions, I have always been aware of their excitement as they respond to the call of God for various forms of missionary service. Overall, they enjoy support from family, friends, and church communities. The outcome of their experiences and exposure to various cultures is normally positive, and the whole adventure enriches their lives and their personal walk with God.

Yet it sometimes seems that those God calls into full-time Christian service at times experience deep and serious testing concerning their faith, commitment, and cross-cultural relationships. It is sometimes exceedingly difficult for missionaries to be separated for extended periods of time from family, church, and their own culture. At times like these, many sincere and committed Christians are challenged concerning their commitment and obedience to the call of God.

From experience, I know that such times can involve deep, heart-wrenching moments, accompanied by intense spiritual conflict as the challenge of being immersed into an alien culture is encountered. On such occasions, there is a need to wrestle in prayer against invisible spiritual powers that are having a negative influence upon those called of God. It is my opinion that Christian workers who do not travail in prayer can be in danger of accusing their fellow workers of causing their struggles.

I have noticed that most, if not all Christians who decide to follow the call of Jesus into other cultures have to make decisions affecting their children, their parents, members of their teams, and even the churches that sent them; and I can assure you—some of those decisions hurt!

Jesus made this point in Matthew 10:36 by making it abundantly clear that those who respond to His call in a lifetime commitment to missionary service must be willing to take up their cross and leave parents and even children, for the sake of the gospel. The wounds of many missionaries, who have served God among the nations of the world, run deep and sometimes they are left with questions that are never answered. Is it right to send our children to a boarding school in the western world while serving God in Africa? Is it right to observe parasites crawling out of the mouths of our children as they slept? Is it right having to remove tumble fly lava from their bodies? Is it right to leave aging parents in our homeland while serving God in foreign places? Is it right that other missionaries should hold me responsible for their personal and cross-cultural grievances? Is it right that our missionary friends were used as human shields by the rebels only to be shot dead by army personnel? Is it right to live in substandard conditions for the sake of proclaiming the gospel?

The list can go on and on, and questions raised as to the rights or wrongs of those questions may never be answered. Nevertheless one overriding factor remains as to why, as a missionary, I should endure the challenge, the pain, the questions, the heartache. That is, a very clear call of God on my life. If I am to accomplish His purposes for my life, I must have complete and utter faith in Him, His call, His power to care for me and the family, and His provision to meet our every need. I can categorically state that our God never forsook us or failed us, regardless of every challenge that confronted us.

This was particularly true for us as missionaries, soon after our third child, Beverley Anne, was born in Scotland. Like her sisters, she was beautiful. We were living in a basement apartment at the time of her birth, and she was a welcome addition to our family. Her mother in particular, loved to wheel her around Aberdeen, also known as the Granite City, in a bright red and silver chrome perambulator. Most mothers love to show off their children, and there was no better way of doing it than in our pram.

Before embarking as a family on a four-year term of service into tropical Africa, in which we would be experiencing some degree of isolation from our homeland, we needed to know that our parents were cared for and, most importantly to us, our three daughters would be safe. Having lived in West Africa for a few years, we were already aware of the risks and dangers that can arise from tropical diseases, coups, robbers, substandard medical facilities and, for the children, educational challenges. Fortunately, we already knew several good doctors, some of whom were themselves missionaries.

Nevertheless, when faced with a challenging situation in Christian service, it is not always easy to sing such songs as "All for Jesus I Surrender." At our wedding service, family and guests sang along with us in faith and sincerity: "I do not know the way ahead, the path I cannot see, but one stands by to be my guide He'll show the way to me." Even before our wedding day, my wife to be and I chose to place God's call above all other responsibilities, by giving it first place in our lives.

Now, as we prepared for another four-year term of service in tropical Africa, we were going to have to trust God with whatever challenges we encountered, and for every need we required. Having been involved in international mission activities from before our wedding day, it was relatively easy on the day we were married to declare that we were going to follow Jesus together throughout our lifetimes. Several years later, as we neared the eve of our departure, that decision was about to be severely tested, especially as it involved our children.

Just weeks before our planned departure to Sierra Leone, we encountered a major reason for *not* going to Africa, except for a very clear call from God. Little did we know at the time that we were standing on the threshold of the greatest challenge we would ever encounter as a family, in which we would discover that only God's miracle power could help us.

Having spent several months working in a Christian bookshop in Aberdeen as part of our prescribed training, and where our third child was born, it was possible to wheel all three children together in our very smart pram.

From Aberdeen, the mission sent us to Norwich, in England, to complete our training and to be instructed in further aspects of Christian literature distribution. It was in the city of Norwich that we encountered the greatest of all challenges – a challenge that not only took me to the very edge of rejecting the call of God, but that also could have been a reason for walking away from every form of Christian activity.

Sometimes it seems to me that Satan has God's permission to use physical events, as with the story of Job in the Bible. In his diabolical attempts to destroy God's spiritual purposes in our lives, he will do everything he can to prevent us from fulfilling God's will, and sometimes he seems to have God's permission to do more than we can endure or understand.

With this concept in mind, I share a very personal incident that involved the deepest of all my inner struggles and where I had to respond to the hardest question Jesus ever asked Peter. Three times in John's Gospel chapter 21:15-19, Jesus tests Peter, and with which

He seemed to be testing me. The question Jesus put to Peter, which seemed appropriate to me at that time was, "Do you love me, and if so, to what level?"

As a family of five living in Norwich, our temporary accommodation was restricted to just one room. Obviously, this was not easy, but it was all part of the training that the mission set for us, so we accepted it as such.

Towards the end of our time in Norwich, an occasion arose when it was necessary for both Sylvia and me, as parents, to leave the room for just a few moments. Having checked them, it seemed to us that our three children were safe and secure to be alone briefly.

Nevertheless, upon returning to our room, we discovered one of them happily chewing the last of a packet of medical tablets that had been left on the table. Although thankful to have seen what had happened, we considered it best to take her to the hospital for medical advice. Having shown the bottle containing the remaining tablets to the hospital team, they decided the safest course of action was for our daughter to have her stomach pumped to ensure that no harm would incur.

The next day, whilst I was preparing to make a cup of tea, our second daughter grabbed the cable of the electric kettle in which the water had reached boiling point, and pulled the kettle off the shelf, covering her with scalding water. She was still screaming as we rushed her to the same hospital we had been at the previous day. The staff informed us that the scalding was so severe she would need to be retained in hospital for several days and placed in an air-purified cot. We were devastated!

The following day, we were back in our single room, where we still needed to boil water. It was with great care that we immediately placed the kettle outside the room after use.

Unfortunately, in the few seconds it took to place the kettle outside the door, our third daughter had pulled the live cable down from the shelf and was happily chewing on the end of it (the plug socket did not have an off and on switch). In one stride, I crossed the room and snatched the cable from her mouth and threw it out of the room.

By this time, everything was just too much. I was overwhelmed with grief, anger, and resentment. Self-condemnation was rampant, and I blamed myself for not seeing, anticipating, or avoiding all these possible dangers. I then blamed the mission for the cramped conditions in which we were compelled to live, and even more concerning, I blamed God for not caring enough for my children.

I began questioning myself about the possibility that I had been misguided concerning all this so-called sacrificial Christian missionary activity. I was furious, thinking that God might have permitted dark and evil forces to hurt my children. Quitting this whole mission malarkey was now a real possibility. I now wanted to leave the mission and was seriously considering returning to employment within the building trade.

Over the next week, we visited our daughter in hospital every day, but the blistered and shredded skin showed no signs of healing. Her physical pain was matched only by our psychological pain. Whatever the outcome, Africa was now firmly on the back burner until all these issues had been resolved, and even then, thoughts of not returning to Africa strongly lingered in my mind.

Every day, Sylvia went to the hospital as normal. Then a few days later, she was informed that within two days the surgeons were planning to take a slither of skin from her to graft onto our baby's little foot. That same evening, we reported to our supporting churches all that had happened. Amazingly, both churches happened to be having special times of prayer on the following day and both promised to offer specific prayer for our injured child.

The following night, we and our churches prayed for the healing for our much-loved child. I still recall the many tears and inner pain of that occasion.

The following morning, Sylvia went to the hospital, knowing that this was the day she would be donating her own skin to aid our child's healing. As she entered the ward, a nurse came skipping towards her, joyfully announcing, "It's come! It's come! You can take your baby home."

"What has come?" inquired Sylvia.

"The skin has come, it's a miracle!" was the reply.

Overnight, as we and the churches prayed, God ensured that our child's own skin should grow back, covering the wounds. How thankful we were to God as we left the hospital later that day, carrying our daughter carefully in our arms.

Three days later, I was watching from the first-floor window of our one-room apartment as Sylvia, with our three children in the pram, waited to cross the busy Princess Street dual carriage area at a pedestrian crossing. All the traffic had come to a standstill, allowing the waiting pedestrians, including my family with the pram, to cross the road.

As I stood watching from the window, a motorcycle came towards them at great speed, the rider seemingly unaware that the traffic had stopped for the pedestrians to cross the road. Passing alongside the stationary traffic, the rider had obviously failed to notice the pram containing our three children on the crossing.

For just a moment, the whole world seemed to freeze before me. I noticed that the faces of most people had turned towards the motorcyclist, who was speeding towards the pram and children.

Then, in just a fraction of a second, it was all over. With absolutely no room to spare, the motorcyclist brushed against the pram and sped on, never to be seen again. I turned from the window, totally stunned. Still shaking with shock and anger, I was unable to move for a moment or two, then having recovered, I rushed down to gather my family together.

For me, this was the last straw. I felt that if God wanted to punish me for something, He had the right to do it; but He had no right to hurt my children.

We left Norwich a few days later with many valid reasons why we should not return to Africa. Yet God was to have the last word. I could see that He had undoubtedly worked a miracle of preservation, healing, and protection that superseded the dangers we had just encountered. Although the events had not been without emotional, physical, or intellectual cost, we had nevertheless survived, and had come through a very challenging situation.

It was the fact that we came through that experience by the grace of God that provided a key to all that was yet before us. During the following few weeks, God's peace was restored and our hearts were at rest. Once again, we responded to the Spirit's call to return to Africa. Our faith in God was rising, as an eagle rises on its wings. God had brought us through a series of life and limb-threatening encounters, and that was the salient issue—God had brought us through the challenging times.

As the Bible records in Isaiah 43:2, *"When you pass through deep waters I will be with you."*

Within just a few weeks of these events, we were on a plane heading for Freetown. Why? Because God had won the day, and as Paul wrote, *"We stopped relying on ourselves and learned to rely only on God. He rescued us from mortal danger, and He will rescue us again. We have placed our confidence in him, and he will continue to rescue us"* 2 Corinthians 1:10 NLT.

Through all those bitter and painful experiences in which we had faced some of the darkest hours of our lives, we discovered that it is better to rely on God than upon our own abilities. I think the choice we made at that time was beautifully explained by a great missionary I knew. He was a gentleman I greatly admired in Liberia.

During his years as a missionary, he had adopted several Liberian orphaned children, raising and caring for them along with his own child. On the day his only birth child graduated from Christian high school in the Ivory Coast, he received an emergency call informing him that she had drowned on the day of her graduation celebration whilst swimming in the Atlantic Ocean.

A little while later, I was able to take the opportunity to visit him and offer my sincere condolences and pray with him. During the visit, we talked about his memories of his daughter and finally when it came time for me to leave, he turned to me and, looking into my eyes, said in perfect calmness, "God knows the intimate details of each one of us. Sometimes He runs His finger up and down the span of our lives and says, 'This is the perfect moment to call this person home' and that is what He did for my daughter. She was called home by God and entered heaven at the perfect moment."

And so it was for us, having decided to entrust our lives and the lives of our family into the hands of the eternal God, even after our painful experiences in Norwich, we knew that we could trust Him no matter what we faced, for God is still running His finger up and down the span of our lives, determining the perfect time for every event.

Chapter 10
Cross-Cultural Friendship

As Christian missionaries living in Sierra Leone, Africa, where I ran a Christian Bookshop, it was our practice to gather together with all our staff at the beginning of each new day to pray. Although every day was committed to God, sometimes we were surprised by an unexpected event. Over the years, I have discovered it is relatively easy to accept those things I expect from God, but I have not always found it so easy to accept all unexpected occasions as being from God. This is especially true concerning some of the people who came to me believing they were God's gift to me.

Although I did not always receive them enthusiastically when we first met, there were some who were undoubtably led of God to work and minister in fellowship with us in the proclamation of the gospel of Jesus Christ. I found accepting them on equal footing within a cross-cultural missionary environment challenging, but when I did accept them, the resulting loyalty and genuine friendship were unbreakable.

By the grace of God, several Africans became more than fellow Christian workers; they became very good friends. They were friends in the way Jesus referred to His friends in John 15:15, which, paraphrased, could read, "I do not consider you to be just workers, because a leader doesn't always confide in his workers. You are my friends and I confide in you as my friends." It has been my privilege to have great African friends who have taken me into their confidence and in whom I have confided and entrusted my life.

As was my normal practice, I was standing at the back of the shop's office when around midmorning a young, well-dressed Sierra Leonean university graduate walked purposefully into the bookstore. She immediately headed towards me like a woman on a mission, which she was!

Without any introduction, she pronounced, "God has told me that I'm to work here." It was not a request; it was a statement of fact and said in such a way that as far as she and God were concerned, everything I was about to hear had already been agreed in heaven. It seemed that my part in her conversation with God was to agree with them.

Having informed me of everything she believed God had revealed to her, she paused, looked at me, and waited.

Her wonderfully blunt presentation had taken me by surprise and for a while I just looked at her, wondering how to respond. In my experience, it was unusual for anyone in Africa to come straight to the point in the way she had just done, and I instinctively knew that I could not respond negatively. The problem I faced was how to say "Yes," for as far as I was concerned, we didn't need any more assistance in the shop at that time, nor could we afford to pay her a wage befitting her qualifications, personality, or ability.

Yet I sensed the Holy Spirit overriding all my objections. I realised that this amazing person standing before me was not seeking employment or inquiring about work; rather, this was a woman of prayer determined to fulfil God's revealed will for her life.

From a practical point of view, I could not see any way to accommodate her proposal, so at that moment, I needed to know how God would have me respond to her.

Claire, as she is named, is one of those amazing people whom God calls to do His will. If, as I believed, she had clearly heard from God on this issue, then I knew she would also understand the prevailing conditions within which she would have to serve Him. I put to her the challenges and restrictions involved in operating a Christian literature distribution centre in West Africa and inquired whether she was still interested.

At the conclusion of our deliberations, we both took a few small steps of faith by saying yes to what we believed was the will of God, and Claire joined our team.

The simple agreement Claire and I made that day proved to be a giant cross-cultural leap of faith for me that led to many blessings. To this day, Claire is an outstanding woman of God, who, although qualified for employment elsewhere, joined the team in our little bookshop, where she proved to be a mighty asset.

God had chosen her along with her husband Wilben, who held a management position with a Freetown company, enabling them to touch the highest echelons of the nation. If, by God's grace, my purpose was just to encourage them by being a stepping-stone to greater things for them, then my contribution to our friendship has been worthwhile. Today these friends are to be numbered with countless other Africans who have accomplished great things for God.

Another remarkable person God brought into my life was Richard Cole. It was Movie, who as our bookmobile operator would sell Bibles and Christian literature throughout Sierra Leone, and who, with his normal overwhelming enthusiasm, suggested to Richard that since he had become a Christian the night before, he could now sell Christian books and Bibles in and around the city of Freetown.

Consequently, the next morning both Movie and Richard, a new convert to Christianity, presented themselves in my office with the proposition that Richard should be entrusted with Christian books, Bibles, and other Christian items to sell in and around offices throughout the city of Freetown. With some reluctance, I agreed to their ideas, knowing that Richard, a man of no fixed address, could be very difficult to trace if he chose not to be found. Nevertheless, on his first day as a Christian bookseller under the supervision of Movie, at least for the first hour, Richard sallied forth into his new adventure of selling Christian literature in government offices, the army barracks, police headquarters, and even in and around the parliament buildings.

Amazingly, and true to his promise, Richard returned at the end of his first day and recounted his experiences to me. Surprisingly, for a young man who had only been a Christian for one day, he had been able to sell a considerable amount of Christian literature and Bibles and his effort was duly rewarded with his share of the profits.

Later, he confided to me that as he left the shop that morning, he was laughing at the stupidity of the white man who had entrusted him with stock to sell. Having at one time been an illegal diamond digger, he had no qualms concerning keeping the money he made. Yet Richard's first day as a colporteur Christian bookseller proved to be the beginning of a remarkable friendship that spanned both our cultures and ideologies.

Richard, like other Africans I knew, could go where I never could, and do things I could never attempt, and be what I could not become. He had the ability to converse in seven local languages; he understood local customs and could relate to influential tribal leaders; and he challenged the police, the army, political representatives, and businesspeople alike on issues of righteousness, justice, and Christianity. During the days to come, he developed the ability to present the gospel of Jesus to everyone he met.

However, at this the end of his first working day, Richard and I chatted for a considerable time. It became apparent that he had nowhere to live, having only access to an old rusty oil drum as his night-time shelter.

That evening I invited him home with me to share the evening meal with my family. I have never seen anyone look as uncomfortable as Richard did that evening. For him, it was the first time entering the home of a white man and he had no concept of European etiquette, as he had only eaten food according to African culture.

Amazingly, he bravely stuck the ordeal out, even though, as he told me later, he felt like running away. Later that evening, he accepted the offer of a room in our annex, where he could spend the night. This arrangement became somewhat permanent, and over the following weeks and months we became co-workers together with Christ. This cross-cultural Christian friendship laid the foundation for many of the extraordinary events that only God could accomplish, resulting in many hundreds of refugees being helped throughout the civil wars with many hearing about Jesus in their own languages.

Sometime later, Richard was invited to transfer from Sierra Leone to Liberia, where the Christian Literature Crusade Bookshop personnel had decided to purchase a bookmobile similar to the one we had in Sierra Leone, for the purpose of distributing Christian literature throughout Liberia. Having had some experience in designing our own, I joined Richard and the team in Monrovia to oversee the construction of a new bookmobile.

Richard, who had grown up on the Sierra Leone/Liberia border, settled quickly into the Liberia culture, and what Movie was to Sierra Leone, Richard became to Liberia. Richard's ministry was remarkable. He was able to encourage church leaders from every stream and branch of Christian denominations. He would visit the homes of politicians and teach the Scriptures to everyone he met. Later he met a wonderful young Liberian widow who agreed to marry him, and from that union a son was born and they named him Philip, or PJ, as he became known.

Unfortunately, following major changes in missionary personnel in Liberia, a temporary replacement missionary, who did not understand African culture or Richard, requested that Richard leave the mission due to their differing opinions on cultural ways. African culture demanded that as I had commissioned him, I alone had the authority to dismiss him. Subsequently, I was sent to Liberia from Sierra Leone to retrieve the bookmobile, account for the stock, dismiss Richard, and hand everything over to a temporary missionary representative.

I will never forget the tears or the pain that flooded my soul that day, nor would I want to, for Richard and I were the best of friends. Not only was the platform of literature distribution taken from Richard, but also the credibility of his powerful ministry that extended throughout the country. The events surrounding Richard's dismissal that day resulted in him becoming discredited in the eyes of the Liberian Christian community.

Some months later, Richard recounted to me the pain of those days. He had returned to his native village in east Liberia and lived in a village hut where he fasted before the Lord for many days seeking God's will for his life. Alone and without support, he waited upon God until God spoke to him. I'm not party to all that God said, but Richard emerged from that time stronger and braver for the Kingdom of God than ever before. Richard feared no one whilst respecting everyone for who they were.

For Richard, his healing began when seeking a sign of divine affirmation of God's calling upon his life. The sign he was looking for came through a very old and frail woman living in a nearby mud hut built in the same forest village where Richard was seeking God. She noticed that Richard had spent many days in intercession, and she was moved by the Spirit of God to provide him with a bowl of soup. That simple act was the beginning of Richard's understanding that God had not and would not desert him.

He discovered that God was able to provide for him as an African in Africa by an African. He learnt that God is as much the God of the African as He is of some Europeans. He later returned to Monrovia stronger and wiser for his bitter experiences and he, along with his wife, was able to support and pray with many church leaders, politicians, and businesspeople. Before the civil war broke out, Richard, along with his wife Yeakah, moved to Freetown, Sierra Leone, and continued their indigenous ministry in the East End of the city.

There are two more friends I must mention. They were just schoolboys who did odd jobs in our garden when we first met. One named himself Philipson and went on to graduate from agricultural college as an adviser, missionary, and pastor to tribal Christian leaders deep within the great Gola Forest. He also established a large church and school in the city of Monrovia.

The other is Isaac, who worked for many years in the Christian Bookshop in Monrovia. During the civil wars, Isaac established a computer training college in Monrovia that gained a reputation for its excellence of training. Over the years, several thousand students graduated with qualifications that secured them employment during the severely challenging circumstances of the civil wars.

These people are my friends with whom I have been able to share my thoughts, pray with, celebrate success with, and help each other. For me, the outstanding virtue that bonded our friendship was the fact that we implicitly trusted each other. There were times throughout the civil war when my life was in their hands, and they never dropped me!

Yet even for the closest of friends, a time can come when we need to walk separate paths. For me, this happened with my friend Richard. Having raised the finances for him to visit the UK, he met a church pastor in London who was able to establish a very powerful and effective ministry for him in Sierra Leone. After assisting countless refugees, Richard, along with his wife Yeakah and later with their son PJ, were able to establish a home in which many ex-child soldiers experienced the rebuilding of their lives. So great was his vision and worldview that many years later, his son, PJ, received the Queen's Commonwealth Young Leaders Award in recognition for equipping over 50,000 people with the lifesaving knowledge of how to deal with Ebola and providing support for more than 8,000 quarantined individuals. PJ had the honour to shake hands with her Majesty at Buckingham Palace in London, on the June 21, 2015.[2]

2   https://www.queensyoungleaders.com/story/pj-cole/

Chapter 11
God Provides During a National Crisis

Following our furlough in 1981, the mission decided we should return to West Africa, but move from Sierra Leone to Liberia. By this time, our fourth child had been born in the country of Wales. At the time of his birth, I was frantically working under our car, attempting to repair the broken suspension system that prevented me from being present.

Unfortunately, I arrived at the hospital a little later than planned and rushed into the ward to see mother and child and, to my great delight, discovered that we now had a son whom we named Richard. How special that moment was. The nurse, knowing we already had three wonderful daughters greeted me and took great pleasure in introducing me to my son. Our family was now complete.

A few weeks later, having arrived back in Africa, Sylvia was giving a children's talk at a special meeting and chose to illustrate the Bible story of Moses in the bulrushes. It was our son Richard who was chosen as the visual aid, and he played his part to perfection as baby Moses. It was so good to have another man about the house.

Having moved from Freetown to Monrovia, although the distance between these two cities is only a couple of hundred miles, the difference in their cultures is noticeable. Sierra Leone, and Freetown in particular, historically reflects a British influence in its education system and matters of government, whilst Monrovia strongly retains its American roots, and the U.S. dollar is still legal tender. There are marked differences between the indigenous people of Sierra Leone, whose fifteen people groups communicate in Creole, and the thirteen tribal groups within Liberia, who communicate in Patois.

There is a gentleness among the peoples of Freetown, many of whom will readily say yes with a smile, but will not necessarily comply with a request or command until a monetary encouragement has been offered to them. For a small price, infringements of law will be waived, which is something very frustrating for those who do not know how the system works.

By comparison, officials in Liberia appear to be rather more aggressive in their attitude towards the public, and sometimes demand a handout before fulfilling their duties or overlooking small infringements of law.

As an Englishman, I found the Liberian culture challenging, whereas in Sierra Leone it was far more laid back. In Sierra Leone, Christian missionaries represent a wide spectrum of British church denominations, whilst in Liberia, missionaries hail mostly from North American churches. The various styles of Christian worship within the two West African countries reflect the traditions of the nations sending and supporting the missionaries. This could be the major reason for the wide variety of Christian worship styles that reflect the sending bases of the missionaries within the two nations.

In both capitals, and indeed throughout the two countries, there is a proliferation of indigenous prophet-led churches that strongly reflect African culture and local Christian traditions whilst maintaining a hint of westernised Christianity. As an Englishman in Africa, I found it interesting to observe that in both countries, among those attending the churches of major denominations, many of their members also frequented these local indigenous churches that remain strongly Africanised. Whilst the established churches remain ritualistic, they seem somewhat powerless against Africa's dark forces, whilst the leaders of the indigenous churches will, for a price, offer prayer for healing, proclaim prophetic utterances, and offer protection against all forms of dark forces.

Although wanting to be non-judgmental concerning my observations, I have always struggled as to how to conduct myself when confronted by these issues, especially when invited to address various congregations that clearly retain what I would consider to be non-Christian practices. In nations where dark forces influence the masses, where the sick and infirm struggle for assistance, and where poverty holds the majority captive, where do the common people turn to for help and assistance? Inevitably, they will seek help from the various forms of traditional medicine men or the so-called Christian prophets.

Having been invited by the mission to move to Liberia, not for the first time, I could think of several reasons for not taking my family there. I needed to consider, among other things, the challenges to my beliefs, the poverty of the nation, the threat of civil disturbances, and the state of disrepair of our accommodation. However, as always, if that was where God wanted us, then that is where we would go. We would just have to trust God to give wisdom and direction concerning the things needed and the things we did not understand.

It just so happened that my travelling to Liberia coincided with the occasion of my fortieth birthday. It had been necessary for me to precede the family on this move in order to prepare our accommodation for their arrival. Also, because of a recent coup attempt, I needed to assess the current political situation. My journey to Liberia necessitated my passing through Sierra Leone to collect documents and make arrangements with the local staff in the Freetown shop to continue the ministry of Christian literature distribution in the capable hands of Claire.

During this short visit to Freetown, my friends threw a surprise birthday party for me, which was great fun and truly a surprise. Sometime later, I came to understand how God used that celebration to make it possible for me to enter Liberia during the civil war, when there was absolutely no means of transportation available to civilians.

Following the few great days in Freetown, I arrived in Monrovia to discover that the situation was not good. Recent and significant political unrest had resulted in a rapid decline in the nation's economy, causing palpable tension among the inhabitants.

Arriving at the mission's accommodation, I discovered it to be in a greater need of repair than expected. Following all the challenging issues we had endured in Freetown, I was not sure it was right to bring my young family into such an unstable situation or rundown accommodation. Due to the country's declining economy and political instability, the distribution of Christian literature throughout the whole of Liberia had been reduced to the point where the organisation was on the edge of bankruptcy.

Although we had experienced several coup attempts in Freetown and endured the challenges of a declining economy in that nation, the situation in Monrovia was much more serious. I felt so uncomfortable with the prevailing situation that I telephoned Sylvia, who was still in the UK, to discuss the matter with her. I suggested that it was not right to bring the family to Liberia at such a time as this.

Her response, as always, was very firm, decisive and blunt. She responded by saying, "God has called us and God will protect us. I am coming." She duly arrived a week later with all four children.

To comprehend the greatness of our God, some understanding of the manifestation of His greatness and grace is required. As European missionaries, our health and security risks were significantly high. All around us were desperately hungry and sick people. As missionaries, we possessed very few of the aids that most other expatriates would consider necessary for life in the tropics, although we ourselves possessed many things our African brothers and sisters were denied.

Our very old car was so full of rust that the road was visible through the floor pan. The electricity supply was spasmodic and soon failed permanently. Our sanitary system required major repairs and was overrun with cockroaches. I discovered bleach does not remove cockroaches, but it does turn them white.

The kitchen was well beyond an acceptable condition. Cupboards and door frames within the property had been eaten by termites. The telephone system had failed. The water supply was being turned off for days at a time until it failed completely. Safe drinking water was fetched from a purified well fifteen miles away, and cooking gas was unavailable, with any cooking being done in the garden over a charcoal fire. Petrol was in short supply, resulting in having to wait in endless queues for just a can full.

Yet despite all these things, God not only provided our every need, He also worked the most amazing works of grace that laid a foundation for greater things to come. No good thing did He withhold from us. God blessed the business of Christian literature distribution and our sales recovered and then remarkably increased. God, at that time, laid it on the hearts of good friends in the UK to come and join us in Liberia. They were brilliant and understood the vision we had for seeing the responsibility of Christian literature distribution firmly placed in the hands of the indigenous people, as it remains to this day.

Yet without God's amazing intervention and provision, we could not have remained in the country. Soon after her arrival, Sylvia was offered a salaried teaching position in an American mission school, enabling three of our children to attend at reduced rates. A little later, I was invited to accept the position of interim pastor of the International Church of Monrovia. The privilege of this responsibility also provided us with a small income, enabling us to purchase a safer car!

The International Church held three services every Sunday. The 8:00 a.m. service attracted mainly local and visiting missionaries, along with a few businesspeople. The 10:30 a.m. main service of the day was broadcast live throughout West Africa. Ministers of state, along with their families, regularly attended this service.

Later, due to these contacts, God was to open amazing opportunities for proclaiming the Christian message, which led to some remarkable experiences. The 6:30pm, evening service provided an opportunity for missionaries of various doctrinal persuasions to fellowship together. Over time, some of the missionaries discovered that not every missionary holding a slightly differing doctrine from their own was a heretic!

My time as interim pastor was very special and a massive privilege. For me, it was an unmerited God appointment that opened many doors of opportunity for the proclamation of the gospel of Christ from city slums to the halls of government. The only qualifications I possessed for this position were "the call of God" and the "enablement of the Holy Spirit." I may not have been man's first choice, but I was God's, and that's all that matters.

Throughout this period of our lives, I had much to learn, the greatest being that God is still the God of miracles. On several occasions, all I could do was to "stand and see the salvation of the Lord."

I have often been surprised at the way some people came to faith in Christ. On one occasion, a young man in his late twenties, who had been attending church for some time, came and informed me that he wanted to be baptised. We chatted over issues relative to his situation and duly set a date that was acceptable to him. During the course of our conversation, he informed me he was a Muslim but wanted to convert to Christianity.

Several issues arose concerning the decision he was about to make, the major one being that before publicly declaring his faith in the Lord Jesus, he needed to know how his Muslim family and village would react to his conversion.

Before publicly committing himself to Jesus Christ through the act of baptism, he decided to return to his distant village and inform his family of his intended conversion. He was fully aware that this might be a life-or-death situation. At best, he would be forbidden to return to his family, but there was also a real possibility that he might suffer the ultimate sacrifice. Following our conversation, he left immediately for his village.

A month or so later, he returned, and we discussed the outcome. He was adamant that he should be baptised on the agreed date, even though he would never be permitted to visit his family or village again. Following his baptism, he would be regarded as a non-person in the eyes of his community.

On the agreed date, he publicly declared his repentance from sin and made a confession of his faith in the saving grace of the Lord Jesus Christ. He then entered the specially prepared baptistery and became a follower of Jesus. He was just one of ten candidates baptised that day, including one of our own daughters. What a very special day!

Along with her friends, Sylvia held regular Bible studies for the wives of high-ranking politicians. They were days of blessing as the women met together to pray over very difficult issues concerning their husbands' lifestyles, including immorality, cancer, and political matters. One of the women, the wife of a Lebanese businessman, attended the local Catholic church and regularly passed on the Bible study notes to her priest.

I discovered this when playing a league squash game against him. During our conversation after the game, I informed him of my vocation, and he said, "Yes, I know who you are because I always receive a copy of your wife's Bible study notes from one of my parishioners, and I approve of them!"

Every Monday evening after sundown, Sylvia and I would go down into the notorious West Point slum area of Monrovia. It is well known as a place of great danger to expatriates, due to the extreme poverty, violence, crime, and prostitution. We met in a church building central to the community and led a Theological Training by Extension course for fifteen pastors. Most of them were leaders of local church fellowships, of which some had very strange practices. When visiting that desperate community, we needed to pass through passageways so narrow that we had to walk sideways between the tin pan shanties with sewer water running at our feet.

We considered it a privilege to be able to meet together in the presence of Jesus with these pastors. The evenings were so very special, and during these times we discovered that these church leaders were totally dedicated to serving their congregations within the squalor that surrounded them.

One evening, we gave the pastors the challenge of demonstrating the Bible truths they were being taught by offering help to local inhabitants in practical ways. The following Monday, the pastors returned with exciting reports of how they had been able to help various people within their communities.

All was well until "Pastor Jimmy" shared his testimony. Apparently, his neighbouring household that lived just a few inches away, separated only by a sheet of corrugated roof pan, had a terrible argument, resulting in a fight. During the fight, the woman had bitten the man's ear off and spat it into the mud.

By this time Jimmy, who had been awakened by the sounds of the fight, entered their shack. When he discovered what had happened, he dropped to the floor and searched for the ear until it was found. He then took the man, along with the ear, to the local hospital.

As Jimmy told his story that night surrounded by extreme poverty, pain, and human darkness, I was reminded again of the needs and situations existing among these people, who are among the poorest in this world. So much of what happens to them is beyond the comprehension of those who live in the developed world. Yet one way or another, the Christian message must be shared and demonstrated with them in the simplest of terms.

These people, through no fault of their own, exist on the outer fringes of society. How are they to understand that there is a God in heaven who really does love them and desires to help them if no one is willing to sit down with them to share the good news? By helping these fifteen pastors, we knew it would have an impact upon fifteen congregations in the midst of one of the world's worst slums. Only eternity will reveal what God accomplished in the lives of those pastors.

Chapter 12

God's Word to the Nation's Leadership

Our four-year term of service in Liberia was drawing to a close. Sylvia, along with the children, had already returned to the UK and now for me, the last few weeks in Monrovia were hectic. Four years in the tropics were taking their toll, and I was now finding it difficult to honour my commitments. I was aware that my afternoon rest periods during the hottest part of the day were considerably longer than before, and my regular games of squash had been completely abandoned.

On one very hot afternoon, whilst resting on my couch under a window, I was disturbed by a commotion on the dusty road just outside my home. Looking through the window, I could see a pitiful gentleman in the middle of the road, screaming at the top of his voice, "Help me, help me, in the name of Jesus, help me!" I could see the man was doubled up with pain and begging for assistance.

Along with other residents, I ran out of the house to help him. As I drew closer, I could see the skin of his back was hanging off in shreds. When questioned, the poor man explained that he had been working daily, unloading ships down in the docks. His job was to carry bags of chemicals off the ship and onto the quayside without wearing any personal protection. The perspiration on his back, mixing with the residue of chemicals of the sacks, was the cause of this horrendous affliction. The poor man had no money to pay for a doctor or to cover the cost of a hospital visit, so he just had to suffer.

Yet again, I experienced God's amazing timing and provision in a way that pertains to this incident. Only four days previously, I had met a Christian doctor from Ghana, who had come to assist the Liberian people. Although employed by the city's hospital, he had also established a first aid room in the centre of our local street market to help the impoverished market people.

Running for my car, I managed to get the suffering man into the front seat and headed for this doctor. We made good time driving through the overcrowded streets and into the market area. Through God's provision, there was space to park the car right outside the doctor's consulting room, which was just a market shack.

To my great relief, I discovered that the doctor was in attendance and was even at that moment free to help the screaming patient. The doctor immediately took the patient into his shack to attend to the man's wounds, refusing to accept the money I offered him. I was deeply moved by all I had just experienced, for even within this impoverished nation, I had discovered that God had people who were willing to do as Jesus did—help the needy people.

During the last few hours of my four-year term of service in Liberia, my thoughts and heart once again were moved with compassion for the crowds swarming around me in their poverty, whilst living with injustice and exploitation. Did Father God have anything else for me to do before I left the country? He sure did!

Amongst the list of responsibilities I had to complete before leaving Liberia, was transferring the running of the bookshop to the incoming missionary, finalising the ministries at the International Church of Monrovia, and preparing for the last few speaking appointments I had accepted. One of those invitations was for a home Bible study, which I was keen to attend as I was friendly with some of the young adults who had invited me. Their enthusiasm over previous times together was so great that I was really looking forward to the event.

On the appropriate evening, I set out to find the home in which the Bible study was to be held. I had been informed that it was in a home I had never visited before, being in an area of Monrovia I did not know too well. This was strange, for although densely populated, Monrovia is not a large city, and I thought I knew most of it.

On this occasion, I had been instructed to drive into a district I was unfamiliar with. Having complied with my instructions, I discovered that in contrast to most of the city's slums, I had entered what was obviously an affluent area. All the properties around me were protected by high block-built walls, complete with iron gates and guards.

Eventually, having made inquiries of the guards as to the whereabouts of the house I was looking for, I was able to leave my vehicle in their protection. A senior representative of the security team then offered to escort me to the home to which I had been invited. Reaching the right address, the security officer passed through its guarded security gates unchallenged and even entered the house without knocking. He then led me straight into the main lounge where the meeting was to be held, which I thought was all very unusual.

Once inside the room, I was struck by its amazing furniture and décor. I was also surprised to discover that it was filled to capacity with well-dressed young adults, of whom just a few were known to me. Following introductions, the evening proved to be one of the most unforgettable times I have ever spent sharing God's Word. The presence of the Lord was tangible in the room, and all who had gathered seemed to hang onto every thought and word that was shared with them.

At the close of the meeting, we all sang together with sincerity, "The presence of the Lord is in this place." Immediately following our time together, a young man approached me and asked if I would lead a lunchtime Bible study in just a few days' time. I agreed, and he went on to explain that it would be held in the Ministry of Foreign Affairs Building on Capitol Hill, situated close to the Presidential Mansion. I returned home that night greatly blessed, for it had been a very special evening.

A few days later, I received a message reminding me that I had agreed to speak at the lunchtime Bible study later that same day. Thinking the meeting would be poorly attended, as these events often are, and that it would possibly be held in some remote back room, I explained that I was not feeling well and was not sure if I could honour the appointment.

The young man to whom I was speaking totally ignored my feeble excuses and with some authority in his voice, insisted that I attend the meeting as arranged and that I should be on time, which in itself was very unusual for that part of Africa. Reluctantly, I assured him that I would be there in time for the meeting.

For this occasion, I had nothing specifically prepared, which was wrong of me and not my normal practice. However, I had some notes I had made by hand a few days earlier concerning a vital subject relevant to the current political situation in Liberia. I believe God had given me some disturbing thoughts concerning Liberia as part of my daily devotions. Although I considered them inappropriate for the Bible study, I thought that since I was going now, within the providence of God, I was compelled to use them, for they were all I had to offer.

The notes were based on a study from Jeremiah 4:6-7a, in which God declared that *"a destroyer of nations has set out."* I coupled this phrase with the Scripture in which God says in Malachi 3:11, *"I will rebuke the devourer for your sakes, So that he will not destroy the fruit of your ground, Nor shall the vine fail to bear fruit for you in the field"* NKJV.

During a previous time of prayer, the Lord had impressed upon my heart that there were six destroyers spoiling the nation of Liberia. The promise of God concerning these spiritual and satanic aggressors was that He would rebuke the destroyers when, or if, the leaders of the nation chose to follow the ways of God. The destroyers of Liberia that came to mind at that time were witchcraft, exploitation, bribery, ignorance, poverty, and sickness, all of which contributed to the poverty, conflict, and divisions among the peoples of the nation.

The young man who had invited me to the Bible study was known to me only by his first name, and he had informed me that he worked at the Ministry of Foreign Affairs. Arriving by taxi, I entered, a little anxiously, through the huge main doors of this magnificent building and approached an enormous desk constructed of teak wood. A well-dressed and apparently well-educated young receptionist inquired as to my business and for a moment, I was at a loss for what to say. Thinking the person who had invited me might only be a janitor, I managed to inform the receptionist that I had come to speak at the lunchtime Bible study.

To my great relief, she instantly knew what I was talking about and instructed one of the nearby fully armed guards to escort me to a waiting room. This room was on the top floor of the building and accessible only by climbing multiple flights of stairs, the elevator being out of order.

Having reached the top floor, the guard showed me into a large, almost empty waiting room and led me to the only seat in the room, which was a hard wooden chair. Following the unexpected magnificence and unusual efficiency I had just experienced upon entering the building, I was now feeling underdressed, scruffy and in need of a shave, whilst continuing to struggle with a hint of one of Liberia's many fevers. At that moment, I was wishing I had not accepted the invitation.

Having been alone in the room for what seemed a considerable length of time, a side door suddenly opened and in strode a well-dressed gentleman. He walked purposefully over to where I was sitting, warmly shook my hand Liberian style, and to my surprise, informed me that he was the person who had invited me to the Bible study. Having greeted each other, he continued to inform me that the banquet was ready.

I felt a shock go through me; I paused. "Banquet?" I said. "What banquet?"

He responded by informing me that he had invited ministers of state, ambassadors from foreign embassies, government officials, and a few friends to attend a lunchtime meeting in the banqueting hall. He then added, "If you're ready, we will go down."

It was obvious by this time, even to me, that the person who had invited me to speak was definitely not the janitor; rather, he was the Minister of Foreign Affairs!

I proceeded to follow him as he led the way back down the stairs and into a vast auditorium that was about half full, which looked more like a theatre than a banquet hall. I had no choice but to follow him, and he led me to the front of the building and up onto the stage, where he introduced me to the invited guests.

Introductions over, I turned to my celebrity host and inquired as to what he wanted me to do. His response was that I should share whatever word God had given me for this occasion. Unable to think of any relevant response to this whole affair, I requested that he stand next to me on stage while I spoke.

Following earnest prayer, I began to address the assembled dignitaries with the word God had placed upon my heart from Jeremiah just a few days earlier. I outlined what I considered to be the destroyers of Liberia, realising, even as I spoke, the relevance this word from God meant to the assembled government officials and their guests.

With the message concluded, I then asked my host what I should do. His surprising response was that I should invite those who believed God had spoken to them to come forward for prayer. With some reluctance, I followed his suggestion and as I did, it seemed that at least half the assembled dignitaries came forward.

I had no alterative than to take the time to pray with, and for, each one of those who had responded. As I worked my way down the prayer line, it became obvious to me that most, if not all of those assembled in the auditorium that lunchtime, knew much more concerning the horrendous political events unfolding on the nation's borders than the people living on the streets of the capital did, including myself. Even as I was addressing government officials in the capital's auditorium, the bloodletting satanic warlord, Charles Taylor, along with his hired mercenaries, had slowly begun to enter Liberia from the Ivory Coast. The bloodletting had begun. My host, being the nephew of Charles Taylor, must have known what was happening.

I sometimes wonder just how much my host knew concerning his uncle, Charles Taylor. Taylor had supposedly "escaped" from a prison in the USA, and having acquired vast amounts of funding, had recruited an army of mercenaries. Following military training in North Africa, he was, at the very time I was addressing the politicians and ambassadors, standing at the borders of the Liberian nation. He had already begun to unleash the powers of hell upon a people overrun by witchcraft, blood covenants, corruption, and greed, which God had promised to deliver His people from if they would seek His face.

I fully believe without any reservation that both my host and his wife were and are sincere godly people, who fully believe in the saving grace of the Lord Jesus Christ. I also believe that God placed him in the role of the country's vice president, where he was able to manifest a degree of God's grace and favour to the nation. I don't know how much he knew about his uncle at that time, but I do know what happened in Liberia over the following years, because God opened the way for me to make several visits throughout the rebellion. I saw for myself the outcome of a nation overrun by the six destroyers, and it was heart-breaking. Only God has the power to rebuke the evil destroyers that entered Liberia that day.

As a result of the Liberia civil wars that raged over a period of fourteen years from 1989 until 1997, an estimated 150,000 people were killed and thousands more became refugees. Many of the Liberian people fled into the jungles whilst others escaped on ships. Although thousands reached the relative safety of refugee camps, many others were captured by the rebels and the treatment they received was atrocious. Women were raped, mutilated, and displaced; most male captives were randomly used as articles of sport.

According to the information I was given, many of the men and women throughout the country, from every tribe, were forced to join the rebellion or be killed. Thousands of rebels were only children, most of whom had been forced to murder a close relative. In it all, witchcraft was rampant.

Yet through those days of living hell, many Christians stood firm in their witness to the Lord Jesus Christ, and I have the privilege of calling them my friends.

Chapter 13
God's Miraculous Provision

Our four-year term as missionaries to Libera was complete. We had already moved out of the mission accommodation, which was now occupied by our replacement, an American missionary. Sylvia and the children were in Belfast, staying in her mother's house, with the task of reintegrating our children back into British culture.

Now that the children were all four years older, they were hardly recognised by family and friends. There was a lot of catching up to do with all our relatives, both in Ireland and England. We were shortly going to have to make some big and difficult family decisions that would have a bearing on our children's education, our employment, location, and what church we would be associated with.

As a family unit, we were now too large and noisy to move in with grandparents, so our immediate future was unknown. Because these issues were of a concern to us before leaving Liberia, Sylvia, in particular, was moved to pray concerning our future and laid before the Lord her requests concerning the choices we should make.

In summary, her prayer was, "Lord, when we return to the UK we will need a large four-bedroomed house. It will need to be located near a London airport so that our friends from Africa can come and visit us. It must have a large and safe garden for the children to play in, preferably with trees to climb and where swings can be hung. It will need to be close to a Christian doctor who understands tropical diseases, be near a school within walking distance from the house, and we will need a regular income."

Despite this request being rather more than I could ask or believe, I managed to add an "amen," and within just a few hours, the family had left for the UK.

With the family back in Belfast, I spent my last Sunday in Liberia speaking at the International Church of Monrovia. The day finished with sharing a wonderful cake made for my farewell. Then, for the last three days, I moved into the home of friends who graciously had invited me to stay with them. Both he and his wife had regularly attended our Tuesday evening Bible study and were employed by the American Customs Department as advisers to Liberian aviation authorities. His work with the US government provided him with the privilege of having a mobile telephone that included an international connection ability. He kindly offered me limited access to this mobile phone with which I was able to make and receive calls from Sylvia, now living in Belfast.

At the end of my last Sunday evening in Liberia, my friend informed me that Sylvia would be calling me on his international mobile phone later that evening. Around 10 p.m. the phone rang and it was Sylvia. My friend passed me his phone and at the sound of her voice, I welled up for a few moments, leaving me feeling a bit choked.

But despite the overwhelming emotion of the moment, she managed to inform me that a pastor from a church in Henley-on-Thames wanted to meet me when I arrived by plane at 6:00 in the morning in two days' time. I asked her why, but she had no idea. We had only met this pastor twice previously and I could not think of any reason why he would want to leave his home at 4 a.m. just to meet me at the airport.

Thirty hours after receiving that phone call from Sylvia, I disembarked from the African night flight at Gatwick Airport. It was just six o'clock in the morning and, having very little luggage, I quickly cleared customs and immigration and entered the arrivals hall. True to his word, Pastor Frank was there, waiting at the arrivals barrier with his companion, the church secretary. We greeted each other with typical British reserve and went for a cup of tea, to which I added a dash of fresh milk for the first time in four years. Of course I did—I was back in the UK!

Following an acceptable British jet-lagged time (never practised in Liberia), I enquired as to why he had come to meet me.

His surprising answer was, "I don't know!"

I thought Liberia was the land of the unexpected, but his reply, so early in the morning, was truly remarkable. I pondered his response and I suppose I looked a bit blank. So, Pastor Frank continued by saying that God had told the church to give us, a family of six, a year's rest.

I was truly startled at this unexpected news, so I asked, "What does that mean?"

"Not sure," was his reply. "Do you have anywhere to live?"

I replied, "Right now, we have nowhere to live, and we own nothing."

"Then I had better take to you to the town of Henley-on-Thames in Oxfordshire where our church is located," was his amazing response.

I don't think it takes much imagination for anyone to realise the impact of leaving an impoverished, desperate nation on the verge of civil war, and moving into the tranquil, established, and very British Henley-on-Thames. The contrast was nothing short of mind-blowing!

Within just two hours of arriving back in the UK, Pastor Frank was taking me around Henley for the purpose of viewing houses that were potentially suitable for our accommodation. On our first foray, nothing stood out as being the right place for us. I think the reason was that I was finding it very challenging to view our immediate needs through western eyes. Everything we looked at was so neat and tidy and costing well beyond anything my imagination could envisage, expect, or financially afford.

At midday, we paused our house-hunting for lunch, as we were not making much progress. This gave me an opportunity to assess everything that was happening around me. It was all so very bewildering. Just twenty-four hours previously, I had been standing in the midday sun surrounded by immense poverty, deeply concerned over increasing political unrest, and watching the infrastructure of a nation noticeably collapsing day by day.

Now, I was looking at houses to rent in cool, calm, laid-back Henley-on-Thames that would cost more in a month than anything in Liberia would cost in a year! I was struggling to accept the reality of everything I was experiencing.

Following lunch, Pastor Frank drove me to a village just a few miles outside of Henley, where a housing agent had invited us to view a modern four-bedroom house on the outskirts of the village, that had just that morning come onto the market. The property I was viewing stood in its own spacious grounds, had a large garden with trees to climb, with plenty of room for swings. The local doctors were Christians and understood tropical diseases.

A secondary modern school was within easy walking distance from the house, and the house itself was suitable for offering hospitality to visiting friends from foreign places. The description of this property I was looking at in a village close to Henley fulfilled every detail of Sylvia's prayer that she had offered to God just a few days previously in Liberia.

What an amazing God!

In addition to the generous provision of a place to live, Pastor Frank then informed us that we were going to receive a monthly allowance to cover all our needs. How good is our God and how faithful are His saints.

Our hearts remain filled with appreciation for all who were involved in what to us was nothing short of a miracle. We remain grateful to the faithful God of love, even to this day. Our God has never failed to provide our every need in every situation we have confronted, and this was a major one that God sorted in eight hours!

On the evening of the same day that I returned to the UK, having been provided with a house, I caught a train from Reading to visit my parents living in Shrewsbury. As I was sharing with my parents, the news concerning the wonderful provision of a house for us as a family, provided by the local Baptist church, I received a phone call to say that the Henley church was now renting the property and we could move in whenever we wanted.

The following day, with help from a local Christian businessman, God provided us with a vehicle, which I immediately booked onto the Irish car ferry, and a day later, I sailed from Stranraer to Belfast to be reunited with my family. It was a miracle of God's grace and love. He had brought us out of Africa with all our worldly possessions packed in small suitcases, had made us the possessors of everything necessary for life in Henley-on-Thames within twenty-four hours of my arrival back in the UK!

Arriving back in Belfast, it was good to be reunited with the family, whom I hadn't seen for a short while. I also had the opportunity to meet the other members of the family I had not seen in four years. Just a few days before arriving in Belfast, Sylvia's mother had moved into a senior citizens' home and kindly permitted us the use of her house. Whilst we were staying in her home, she offered us all her furniture, which we sent to Henley in a lorry a few days later.

Within a week of our arriving in the UK, God had answered every prayer, supplied every need, and fully equipped us for life back in the UK.

Having met and spent time with our Irish family, we travelled back from Belfast to Henley and arrived at our new home for the first time a few days later. After the very long drive and feeling extremely tired, we arrived just in time to see the lorry containing our furniture turn into our driveway and the family hadn't even seen the house yet. Because we wanted to sleep in our own beds in our own home that night, we immediately set to work unloading the lorry.

Night had fallen before we finished unloading, and during the last stages of the task, a large people carrier turned into our driveway. We stopped what we were doing and watched in amazement as six Americans stepped out of the vehicle and greeted us. They were missionary friends from Liberia, and they reminded us of what we had said to them: "If you want to visit the UK, just turn up at our doorstep."

Taking us at our word, they had done just that! So, we said, "If you want to spend the night, you will need to help us finish unloading this lorry."

They willingly agreed, and then spent a night or two with us in our new house. How can I ever doubt the God in whom we trust who, within seven days of our arrival back in the UK, had answered every detail of Sylvia's prayer and had wonderfully, faithfully, and safely installed us in our new home.

Chapter 14

From Building Houses to Building People

Our time in Henley was very special and we remain forever grateful for all the generous hospitality the church there offered us. With their help, our children lost their Afro-American accents and within days integrated back into the British way of life. Inevitably, the day came when we needed to move on from the church and continue with the plans God had for us.

As a first step, I returned to being self-employed in the building trade. In many ways, this could be regarded as being a backward move spiritually, as I no longer retained the status of being a missionary or a pastor within the church. Once again, I was just a normal working husband seeking to earn a decent wage for my family.

I'm not sure whether God has a sense of humour or not, but the very first task I was offered as a builder was in Henley-on-Thames at the house of the assistant pastor of the church I had just left. The sewer pipes connected to his toilet system had become blocked, causing a risk of a flood inside his home. In seeking to discover where the blockage was, it was necessary for me to lie down flat on the floor and lower my head into the manhole of his house.

Whilst in that abominable situation, I clearly remember praying, "Lord, thank You for the high moments of life during which You have made great and wonderful provision; right now, I thank You for this, the lowest of all low moments with my head hanging down inside the pastor's sewer system. God, You are the great provider; whatever situation I find myself in, I will praise Your holy name! Glory be to God in the highest!"

I remained very busy in the building trade and never lost a day's work thanks to the many Christian contacts I had. But even while I worked in my business, the atrocities occurring in the West African rebellion were increasing. Sometimes I would receive telephone calls from Freetown or Monrovia, updating me on the situation concerning the Christians I knew, and they were all requesting my help.

It was in response to these requests that a small group of us began sending aid to West Africa as God would provide for us. Our first shipment consisted of just six tightly packed barrels of the items that had been requested. Then, as God provided, we progressed in the quality and quantity of goods until we were sending whole containers of aid. Each one of those containers was a miracle of God's love and provision.

I never had to make requests for goods or finances, as supplies of every description flooded in, including vehicles, generators, clothing, educational supplies, hospital beds, tools, bicycles, and eventually, computers.

As each of the fully loaded containers was shipped to West Africa, so the finances for the shipping and landing costs were provided. The abundance of support being received became so great that it became necessary for me to begin visiting West Africa on a regular basis. These were times for fellowship, planning, and the sharing of finances to cover all the costs payable in Sierra Leone and Liberia for bringing the relief goods into those countries, as well as supporting the local leaders.

So much of my time had now become devoted to the administration of sending aid, along with the many visits I was making to West Africa, that my self-employment began to suffer. The tension between giving time to my employment and my commitment to my suffering friends came to a head on the morning I discovered a thousand-pound bank draft on the doormat of my home, with absolutely no indication of where it had come from.

When this happened a second time, it came to the notice of Her Majesty's tax inspectors. As a result, I was summoned into their office to be questioned extensively as to where I had obtained the money. They had great difficulty accepting my explanation as I informed them that I had found it on my doorstep! Their investigation intensified until, in exasperation, I finally burst out saying that I could not force God to write a receipt in the clouds with His finger just for their benefit. I never heard from them again!

By this time, it was becoming clear that my employment in the building trade was coming to an end, but I did not yet know what the next step of God's plan for me was. However, it was abundantly clear that we needed to move from the amazing property God had provided for us into cheaper accommodation.

As a result, and through the generosity of friends, we were offered the accommodation we needed and subsequently moved to another village, where we became part of the local church fellowship. I was then able to continue visiting West Africa on a regular basis.

So much of my time was now being given to my friends in West Africa that once again, we realised that we would not be able to afford to live even in the temporary, cheaper rented accommodation we now had.

Although God had opened the floodgates of generosity with funds for the relief of many in the war zone, we, personally, were finding it very difficult, as I was receiving little or no income from my employment activities. We just could not afford to remain in our current situation even though Sylvia was employed as a schoolteacher and the children were in full-time education.

Once again, our amazing God, who works all things together for good to them that love Him, made an unexpected provision. By this time, our children had graduated from their universities and were seeking employment. Wonderfully, one of our daughters was offered work with an international airline as an airline hostess. This entitled her to discounted flight tickets that included family members. This provision enabled me to travel business class to various destinations in West Africa, as I carried funds in support of our African brothers and sisters. It also meant that I was exposed firsthand to their horrendous experiences.

The pressure was now getting to me, so I suggested to Sylvia that we should move away from our current address into a location where renting property would be much cheaper. With typical Irish resolve, and in that tone of voice that does not invite debate, her reply once again was, "God brought us here; God will keep us here."

She then went on to inform me that she had heard of a small country church that had a vacancy for a minister. Amazingly, this little church was only a mile or so from where we first lived, but we had never seen or even known about it.

On the strength of what we had heard, we wrote a letter to the members of Peppard Congregational Church, inquiring as to their needs for a minister and our suitability for fulfilling that role. After diligent searching and making inquiries, we discovered where the church was located and who the church secretary was.

Arrangements were quickly made for us to meet her, and we soon went to visit her in her beautiful country cottage, where we had been invited for afternoon tea. Duly arriving at the appointed time, we were amazed at the multitude of knickknacks in this old-world cottage, along with the hospitality being offered to us.

We spent a considerable amount of time with her that afternoon, partly because she was very hard of hearing, but also because of the time needed for her to regale us with her multitude of stories from her vast local knowledge and life experiences.

Eventually, she came to understand that the reason for our visit concerned the vacant pastorate of the church. She promised to talk to the other members about it, so we left a letter of introduction with her and returned to our home.

Within a couple of weeks, the members of the church responded to my letter by inviting me to officiate at their once-a-week service, held at three o'clock on Sunday afternoons.

Having accepted the invitation, I duly arrived a little before service time and entered the sanctuary through a large, heavily studded side door, complete with a huge ringed door handle. Once inside, I had time to look around and it became immediately obvious to me that nothing in this much-loved church had been altered for almost two hundred years. It still contained most of its original furniture.

At the back of the church there was a small balcony, accessible only by ascending the narrowest of all stairways. The balcony itself contained its original tiny fitted narrow benches, which for those sitting on them, gave the sensation that they were about to topple over the balcony and onto the floor below! In the main sanctuary, handmade pews shone deeply from years of polishing.

Dominating the front of the church and situated to one side of the platform, was a great raised ornate pulpit where the preacher traditionally would need to ascend three steps to address the congregation. Once positioned in the pulpit, the preacher stood midway between the main body of the church and the balcony, from where he could observe all the parishioners.

At the other end of the platform stood a very ancient electric organ that looked like it needed a bit of care and attention. Extensions had been added to both sides of the church. The larger of the two extensions had at one time been the original village primary school. This old school room was separated from the sanctuary by a folding screen, in which small beautifully hand-painted windows had been installed.

By now, the time for the service was approaching, but being unfamiliar with Congregationalism, I stood at the back of the sanctuary near the side door, not quite knowing what to do with myself. Although I had received a polite nod from all nine members who entered, no one actually spoke to me.

Standing at the door, I noticed that as each of the nine members entered, they headed straight to what I assumed was their usual seat, and as they did so, each member snapped a pound coin down on the pew before them, ready for the collection. A very strange tradition!

Whilst I was pondering the rituals of this very small and aging congregation, the visiting organist suddenly struck up a strident melody with great enthusiasm in a style maintained throughout the service. He drowned out all of the small congregation's attempts at singing. It possibly also explained the condition of the organ, which was in a state of disrepair, extremely loud, hard on the ears of the congregation, and obviously nearing the end of its usefulness as a musical instrument.

I assumed, as he reached a blasting crescendo, that this was a signal for me to take my place on the platform. I chose to stand adjacent to the communion table and to lead the service in a plain and simple manner according to my understanding of nonconformist ways. More importantly, I was able to avoid the necessity of climbing into the pulpit and then having to look down on the nine members.

At the close of the service, I walked to the back of the church and stood by the great door, determined to shake everyone's hand as they left the service. As I did so, every member of the congregation gave me a little smile along with a nod of the head. It seemed obvious to me that there was no clear leader among the group, but I guessed they would all be discussing their thoughts concerning me.

On the whole, I thought everything went well. Next day, I departed for Africa, pondering over the enormity of contrasts between various Christian styles of worship. I recalled the quiet, reflective attitude displayed by the nine members of the chapel I had just visited, knowing that in just a few hours I would be expected to join the flamboyant exuberance of the dancing, singing, and clapping of hands by the members of an enormous African congregation. I assumed it would be an impossibility to unite these two styles of worship in this life and wondered what style of worship will be adopted in heaven when we all see Jesus!

Upon my return from the challenging and desperate situation in Sierra Leone, there was a letter waiting for me from the members of the Congregational church. The congregation had reached the unanimous decision of inviting me to be their minister.

Within just a few days, we moved from our current accommodation into the manse, which, along with the grounds, was in desperate need of renovation. Later, we discovered that the church, having been built two hundred years previously, was at the time of construction, not permitted by law to be seen from the public highway, which is why we had never noticed it before.

The history of the building of the church is of great interest to me, for I believe that two hundred years previously, a village prayer group had met monthly, seeking God's mercy and blessing on the neighbourhood. Members of this group were particularly concerned over what was known as "The Peppard Revels," which were held once a year on a public holiday.

These revels were riotous and traditionally held during the Easter period and were renowned for their drunkenness and organised cudgel fighting. Apparently, the winner of a cudgel fight was declared when the skull of his opponent was split open. The winner was then duly rewarded with one shilling as his prize. During those times, the small prayer group sought the promises of God for the area in which they were located, and prayed earnestly about their concern over the revels.

Every Easter during the revels, they preached the gospel of Christ from the back of a horse-drawn cart to the revelling crowds. This prayer group later saw the fulfilment of their vision by the building of the little church. I believe that the church was built upon the prayers of people and the promises of God where, two hundred years later, I was called to be the minister. Amazingly, it seemed that I was chosen of God to experience the blessing of near revival, and the growth of the membership from 9 to 130 members in answer to the prayers made and the promises received by that prayer group.

As a family, we moved into the manse and quickly settled into our new accommodation. Along with our four children, and having been joined by a few friends, we almost doubled the size of the congregation the day we arrived. My objective was just to care for this aging congregation and, as part of that, I visited each member in his or her home most weeks. This involved chatting with them concerning their memories and expectations over the drinking of much tea from strange cups.

Back at the church, I was kept very busy with a great deal of practical work that needed to be accomplished around the grounds, in the graveyard, and in the manse. As a result, the congregation was happy to see the premises and grounds cared for, and we were thankful for a place to live.

Sylvia continued her employment as a schoolteacher and the children with their further education. I only had the responsibility of one short afternoon service each week, which was not too much of a challenge, but unknown to us, God was about to step in once again and surprise us with the unexpected.

As time passed, we asked the members of the church for permission to hold a Sunday morning service for village people who could not attend the afternoon one. The members agreed and on our first Sunday morning, eighteen people attended.

We chose to meet informally in the schoolroom that had been added to the church, rather than in the sanctuary. During our time together on that first Sunday, I sensed the Spirit of God impressing upon me that we would never see fewer people attending the morning service than were there that first morning.

And so it was, that this little unobtrusive church nestled in the Oxfordshire Chilterns, having only nine elderly members, began to reap the results of historical prayers offered by saints of God two hundred years ago. The scene was set for us as a family to experience that which God had ordained for the future.

During the next few years, the fellowship expanded to a congregation of around a hundred and thirty, with many more people attending the services. Local people came to Christ for salvation with many being baptised. The dividing screen between the school room and the sanctuary was folded back, and on some Sundays, the gathered congregation was so great that there was standing room only. People were now sitting on the window ledges, up the stairs, in the balcony, and on the carpeted floor. This was not due to the skill of the minister, but totally due to the grace of God, who had great plans for what was now a significant congregation, possibly in response to the prayers made over two hundred years ago.

Although the church was growing steadily, I knew the congregation still could not afford even a limited salary for me, although I was receiving some support.

As a result, I considered seeking part-time employment to ease the financial burden on the members. Having discussed and prayed about this issue with my courageous and long-suffering wife, Sylvia, who was still employed part-time as a schoolteacher and supplementing our income, we decided to leave the final decision of what to do until I returned from a pastors' retreat I had been invited to. This retreat, to be held in Wales, was led by a former pastor of mine.

The time spent at the retreat was enriching and beneficial. For me, the whole event came to a climax when the leader invited a young man from his very large church to seek God for a word of encouragement for each of the nine delegates attending.

Amazingly, but maybe not surprisingly, the young man, who knew nothing about my situation, was invited to pray for me. As he stood before me, he simply stated that he believed God was indicating that I should remain as the minister of the church without seeking any other sources of income. As confirmation of this, he indicated that there would be a personal gift designated just for our family and it would be waiting for me when I returned home.

Being a little surprised at this statement, the first thing I enquired about after returning home was if such a gift had arrived. After some discussion, my wife informed me that yes, a small personal gift had arrived in the post that morning from Lebanon. It was from a wonderful Lebanese friend whom we knew from our time in Liberia.

In her letter, she explained how God had awakened her during the night a week previously, requesting her to send us a personal gift of just £5.00. She was somewhat embarrassed by this whole affair, but was sure that this was what God wanted her to do, so she obeyed.

Amazed as she was at this divine instruction, she would have needed to have sent the gift several days before I attended the retreat in order for it to arrive exactly at the right time from Lebanon. In the past, this friend had faithfully attended Bible studies Sylvia led in Liberia.

How amazing are the ways of God and the people He calls to serve Him. Our friend was so greatly encouraged when we telephoned her to inform her of what the gift had meant to us. She was also thrilled to know that she had clearly heard and responded to God.

Life in the church had now become very busy as we continued to send containers of aid, mostly to Sierra Leone. One morning, I received a phone call from Isaac, our co-worker in Liberia. He asked me if it was possible for us to send him five computers. I made what I thought was the right response without making a firm commitment, and pressed on with the duties of the day.

As we sat down for our evening meal around five o'clock that evening, we heard a knocking on our front door. Upon opening the door, an unknown gentleman was standing there and simply said, "I've five computers. Can you use them?"

What an incredible God-ordained moment that was. God had just made another unexpected provision, which, in the days to come, was to lead to what I can only describe as a modern-day miracle.

Over the following days, weeks, months, and years, we received dozens, if not hundreds, of computers. Volunteers with computer knowledge came forward to check, service, and sometimes discard the mountain of computers we received. One of our helpers was employed by the Williams Formula One racing team, and another was a Daily Telegraph reporter. They both offered much time and energy, supporting the miracle of God by sorting through the computers.

With the simplest of humble beginnings, a little computer school, founded by Isaac in a rented room in the local YWCA on the outskirts of Monrovia, was launched using the five second hand computers. Later, God was to provide a suitable building that was gifted to us. It is estimated that over the following years over three thousand Liberian students successfully completed the computer training course; and it all began with the five computers that were offered to us at our front door on the right day at the right time!

The second part of what I consider to be a contemporary miracle of God lies in the abilities of the vast majority of the computer-taught graduates. Most of the graduates were offered employment within the city of Monrovia whilst it was still in a devastated state and where unemployment was rife. Employment for the graduates was possible due to the flood of government officials, peacekeepers, and the non-governmental organisations (NGOs) who, being supported by the international community, all required competent office staff with computer skills.

Even the chairperson of the Senate, who was a guest speaker at one of the computer school's graduation ceremonies, publicly offered immediate employment to the young female graduate leading the ceremony. She was so efficient at chairing that she was instructed to report to the senator's office ready to commence employment the following morning.

Amidst the cheers and celebratory dancing of this typical African graduation occasion, how we all praised God for yet another miracle. What a day that was—what a God we have!

During the years of civil unrest, it was estimated that in the city of Monrovia, for every employed person, up to ten people were fed every day. If that is true, then several thousand people were fed daily through the wages that our graduates earned, which was a provision that only God could make.

Around that time, I was meditating on the words of Jesus as recorded in John's Gospel. Jesus had just fed five thousand men and as His disciples were contemplating all that Jesus had done that day, Jesus turned to them and said, *"I tell you the truth, anyone who believes in me will do the same works I have done, and even greater works, because I am going to be with the Father. You can ask for anything in my name, and I will do it, so that the Son can bring glory to the Father"* John 14:12-13 NLT.

I have always found these amazing words difficult to apply to our world today. Because of war, sickness, famines, and exploitation, multitudes of people are in critical need of daily food. In my simplicity, I said, "Lord, where in the world is this promise being fulfilled?"

I sensed the Holy Spirit responding to my question by indicating that it was happening in Monrovia. I was reminded that what Jesus did on that one occasion had now become a daily event for the hundreds of people who were being fed due to the employment and generosity of the graduates of the Christian Computer Institute. Among them, it is possible that on some days the graduates were providing food for hundreds of people during desperate times throughout the civil wars.

Chapter 15
MV Logos Visits Monrovia

MV Logos, the world's largest floating Christian book exhibition, operated by Operation Mobilisation, normally carried a crew of about four hundred personnel. These were mostly young vibrant Christians from around fifty-five nations, who are willing to share their faith within the ports of the world, and that included Liberia.

I knew the leaders of OM would never endanger the lives of the crew or risk the ship in any hostile areas of the world, but the question concerning a window of opportunity had opened, and a visit to Liberia was being considered as the warlord, Charles Taylor, had become president of the country. From my experiences with this organisation many years previously in Sierra Leone, I knew that concentrated prayer and effort would go into the planning of such a visit, as of all ports to be visited.

The first time I encountered the Operation Mobilisation ship, MV Logos (now decommissioned), was when it visited Freetown. I was deeply impressed by the dependency upon God that was displayed by the forward planning team who lived on our premises. Their task in visiting was to evaluate all prevailing risks and conditions in the country. Only when deemed to be safe would representation be made to the president of the country who, along with the heads of the Christian denominations and organisations, would endorse the visit.

After several coup attempts to overthrow the government in Sierra Leone had failed, suddenly there had been an opportunity for the ship to visit Freetown. Consequently, even though the Sierra Leonean army used excessive amounts of tear gas to restrict the crowds, thousands of Sierra Leoneans were blessed and encouraged during the time the ship was in port.

As a result of this previous encounter, I was excited to hear of the proposal of the Christian Book Ship, now the successor to the original ship Logos II, to visit Liberia. It seemed right to me to respond positively to the invitation I had received to visit and pray with the leadership team on board Logos II whilst moored in Bari, Italy. Having arrived on board, I discovered that the vessel was relatively quiet as most of the crew members were taking a break from their remarkably busy schedules.

Having met the *MV Logos* leaders previously, I knew they would keep the well-being of the ship's company in mind whilst seeking to follow God's will. Therefore, for them to make inquiries concerning a visit to Monrovia during a period of relative calm was not altogether surprising. The question being put to me was whether or not I thought *MV Logos* should include Monrovia on its upcoming African itinerary.

I found it impossible to give a simple yes or no answer to such a question. On the one hand, the ship's visit would provide a once-in-a-lifetime opportunity to encourage and help thousands of Liberians who had already suffered horrendous atrocities due to the filthy civil war. Yet undoubtedly, there were risks surrounding such a visit that needed to be carefully evaluated. When seeking God in prayer concerning what advice to give, three indicators came to mind, which would be normal for the *MV Logos* directors to consider anyway:

If it was God's will for the ship to visit Monrovia, it should be clearly endorsed:

1. Unanimously by church leaders of all denominations.
2. By the Minister of Education, personally guaranteeing the safety of the crew and ship.
3. Personally by the President of Liberia.

These indicators would not be lightly endorsed as they would require serious commitment and support by those holding various offices of authority in Liberia. Although I didn't realise it, the three conditions set for a visit were perfectly timed and were only possible because of what could be regarded as the sovereign intervention of God.

As plans for the timing of the ship's visit were being considered, Liberian President Charles Taylor was in China seeking financial assistance for Liberia. I am sure this was of God, for although Charles Taylor was supposedly religious with some interest in Christianity, he was also deeply embedded in satanic rituals and was somewhat erratic in his behaviour.

The Vice President, acting as President in his absence, was his nephew, Jonathan Taylor. This was the same Jonathan who had invited me to speak at the Ministry of Foreign Affairs meeting some months previously. He was also co-pastor of Monrovia's largest church, along with his wife, who also was an enthusiastic Christian. Not only did she know me, but I knew she would fully support the idea of a visit by *MV Logos*.

The Minister of Education, whose two sons I had baptised some years previously, would sometimes attend a church service with his wife, who was a committed Christian. She occasionally attended the women's prayer group that Sylvia was involved with.

The Minister of Education, one of the original coup leaders, had a part in the overthrow of the previous government and was known to be a very hard man. Fear of him was widespread throughout the city. He had recently fallen out with another very powerful 1980 coup leader, Thomas Quiwonkpa. The disagreement resulted in the two of them engaging in a hand-to-hand fight with knives, within the grounds of the International Church of Monrovia.

Quiwonkpa was slain in the fight, and it is rumoured that parts of his body were used in a witchcraft ritual. If *MV Logos* was to visit the Monrovian port, we were going to need the approval and support of the Minister of Education!

The *MV Logos*, having sailed from Italy, then visited South Wales, where once again I was invited to meet with the ship's leadership. I was informed that a previous decision concerning *MV Logos* visiting Liberia had been negative but had now been reconsidered.

Following times of earnest prayer, Liberia was now on the itinerary as a possible port of call. The leadership agreed to adopt the approval and support of the acting President of the country, Jonathan Taylor, as a sign that such a visit was of God. Accordingly, I made appointments to discuss the matter with the church leaders of Monrovia, the acting President of Liberia, the Minister of Internal Affairs, and the Minister of Education. This made it necessary for me to make plans for an immediate visit to Liberia.

Having arrived in Monrovia, I reflected on the events that had occurred within the shadow of the church where I had once been the interim pastor. The church building itself had been damaged by mortar and gunfire, which caused me to reflect upon the atrocities that had taken place within its vicinity. On previous visits, I had been surprised to see that every palm tree along the beach area had been cut down, totally blocking the road. When enquiring why, I was informed that besides palm trees providing coconuts, palm oil, and dates, there is another edible part of the palm known locally as the palm cabbage, but the tree must be destroyed to obtain its heart.

As I observed the total destruction around me, I wondered whether the nation of Liberia, which had been cut down, would recover if God was to restore the heart of the nation. Would the visit of *MV Logos* be a means of restoration and blessing to this nation in which God would prove to be victorious over the demonic events that had occurred on this site?

The following day, I arrived at the Ministry of Education offices, along with the *MV Logos* representative, where we were made to wait for a considerable time in a small anteroom. During the waiting, I wrestled with my thoughts as I reflected on the possibilities of what the outcome of this visit might be, which might not be pleasant.

Eventually, we were invited into the Minister of Education's office and on sight of us, the Minister immediately rose from behind his desk and headed straight towards me without speaking a word. I knew by reputation that he was armed, and I was somewhat concerned over his reaction at seeing me. As he came within touching distance, he unexpectedly threw himself down at my feet and, without warning, grasped my shoe in the traditional African way of begging forgiveness.

I immediately knew I was out of my depth and totally dependent upon God, into whose hands we had committed ourselves. I could not begin to imagine what might happen next, for there were no guardians of law and order anywhere in Liberia at that time. Every politician did what was right in his own eyes, and that with the power of the gun.

Still stunned by what had occurred, I mumbled something that seemed appropriate in the way of some form of acceptance. Then,

having regained his composure, the Minister of Education returned
to his seat behind his desk.

The outcome of this unexpected behaviour was his assurance to us
that every facility and help would be offered to us for the safety of the
ship and its crew whilst in Monrovia. God had once again ruled and
overruled every action and reaction.

Within this amazing incident, I clearly saw the hand of God, who had
begun to make the visit of *MV Logos* to Liberia a real possibility. As is
written in Deuteronomy 31:8 NLT, *"Do not be afraid or discouraged,
for the Lord will personally go ahead of you. He will be with you; he will
neither fail you nor abandon you."* God had gone ahead of us years
earlier when I had the privilege of baptising this man's two sons. Now,
in the presence of Jesus, who was with us, this demonically motivated
and ritualistic man had bowed his knee to the will of a sovereign God.

Following the amazing, or even miraculous event, we set out to keep
our appointment with the Minister of Tourism and Public Affairs,
for we also needed her consent and cooperation for the ship's visit.
Once again, we had to wait an unreasonable amount of time before
our interview. Eventually, we were invited into her office and as we
entered the spacious room, she stood up from behind her desk and
greeted us by saying, "Hello Pastor."

Taken aback, I enquired how she knew me. Her response was
surprising and embarrassing as she informed me that she had
often attended church service on a Sunday morning as a member
of the congregation and not as a minister of state. Although I was
embarrassed and shocked to see her, I was greeted like a long-lost
friend and assured of her total support for the ship's visit.

From the Ministry of Tourism and Public Affairs, we went to the
office of the Roman Catholic Bishop of West Africa, as we required

the support of every section of the Liberian church for the ship's visit. The Bishop proved to be very accommodating and willingly offered to support the venture wholeheartedly.

Towards the end of our interview, he suddenly turned to me and said, "I know you," as though he had just realised it.

"No, sir," I replied. "We have never met." He persisted with his claim and repeated a second time, "I know you." He was so adamant in his statement that I had to inquire how he knew me. His response revealed yet another amazing way God had already prepared the way for the ship's visit.

"Because," he said, "I used to hurry home after Sunday morning mass just to hear you preach over the radio."

I was dumbstruck! Regardless of all my personal struggles and weaknesses, God had been, and was at work, doing things I could never even begin to imagine. He had forged contacts and opened channels of communication that would be key to the ship's visit long before we needed them. No wonder the Bible records that when God opens a door, no man can shut it, and His angels go before us, making a way where there is no way.

When I returned to the UK, and the ministry of the church, I received confirmation that there was now a strong possibility of the ship including Liberia in its African itinerary. Along with this good news, I was also offered an invitation to visit the *MV Logos* in the port of Recife, Brazil. From there, I was being invited to undertake the African orientation for the whole ship's company as it sailed from Brazil to Benin in West Africa. Thanks again to our daughter's occupation as an air hostess, this was a financial possibility; so, plans were quickly made, and I was soon on my way to Brazil, flying in style.

I had never had the privilege of meeting Latinos before. Their exuberant lifestyle and enthusiasm for God is exhilarating. Everything about them seemed to be upbeat. As the sailing time from South America to West Africa took several days, we had many sessions in preparation for things to come. I enjoyed every minute of them and trust the feeling was mutual.

Having reached West Africa, I left the ship whilst it was in Ghana and returned home for a few weeks before returning with my wife, Sylvia, to re-join the ship in Dahomey. As is to be expected when travelling in West Africa, what can go wrong will go wrong, and our arrival at Dahomey International Airport was no exception. Normally, we would travel in and out of African airports without hindrance, having learnt to follow all form-filling and other procedures to the letter in compliance with local expectations.

On this occasion, however, I failed to notice that Sylvia's Yellow Fever certificate had been stamped with the medical authentication stamp in the wrong place. As we passed through immigration and customs, we waited for the medical officer to check our certificates. His eyes lit up when he immediately noticed the error.

For almost an hour, we argued our case, indicating that we had the correct certification but that the authentication was simply in the wrong place. The officer would not accept our pleadings or explanation; in his view we were easy pickings to receive an unauthorised payment from us.

This whole debacle came to a conclusion when the officer took down an old decrepit medical box from a shelf. From the box he extracted the largest injection needle I have ever seen and began to fill it from a strange-looking bottle containing unknown liquid which had not come from the refrigeration unit. By this time the ship's organiser had joined us and in front of him and for the first time in all the years of travelling in that part of the world, I offered the official what he wanted in the first place—a handout of money.

I felt terrible, an absolute failure until I remembered that God had shown me the difference between extortion and bribery.

A few days later, we sailed from Dahomey to the port of Monrovia, where the entire crew were in an understandable state of excitement.

When the harbour boat drew alongside and the officials came onto the deck, they immediately demanded the surrender of every camera in sight. The onboard euphoria immediately turned from joy to shock, as we realised we were entering into a significantly challenging situation with a mandate to encourage a suffering nation.

MV Logos' visit to Liberia proved to be a time of great blessing in which thousands of people visited the ship. Later, it was most significant to notice that within one hour of the ship's departure, a military crackdown was imposed upon the city with extreme and aggressive policing in which I was stopped and questioned.

For the duration of the ship's visit, there was a time of God's blessing and refreshing in preparation for the waves of hostility, war, torture, and death that were about to be unleashed, in what became known locally as World War Two.

The events that occurred were unparalleled in the country's history. Satanic atrocities were performed by children of nine years and upward. After the heavenly respite of the *MV Logos* visit for a couple of weeks, in which hundreds of people were blessed, all hell broke loose.

Chapter 16
Could Have Done Better

It's strange how the comment inscribed on my final school report caused me so much trouble, not only at the time it was written, but on many occasions later. The comment made by the headmaster read, "Could have done better."

In seeking to help people whose needs were so great that, regardless of how much I accomplished, there was always much more to be done. This situation often caused me to reflect on what more I should be doing. Although amazed at the grace and protection God provided me throughout those dark days of high risk, danger, and decision making, I sometimes think if I had known what I was getting into, not only would I have done things differently; I would possibly have done better—or would I?

Throughout the worst days of the rebellion, it seemed that God opened the gates of heaven, flooding us with a deluge of financial and practical help in support of those in need. I was just the channel God used to bless His people who were caught up in hellish hostilities through no fault of their own.

The problem I struggled with was knowing whom to help, when to help, and how to help. For although I was able to carry significant amounts of funding into the conflict zones, it immediately became insignificant among the hundreds and even thousands of refugees surrounding me.

Sometimes I felt guilty for spending a night in a hotel because the needs around me were so great. At such times, it was all too easy to have feelings of condemnation for what I hadn't accomplished, rather than just trusting that God was leading me to those He wanted me to help. It was sometimes difficult to shake off the feeling of guilt, thinking I was not doing enough to help the people around me. At such times, it was vital that I kept my eyes on God, recognised the opportunities He was giving and acknowledged the miraculous provision He was making. I then had to deliberately refuse all forms of guilt and condemnation arising from the thought that I "could have done better."

It is impossible to explain the moving of the Holy Spirit in a person's life, for it is as gentle moving as the autumn wind stirring fallen leaves in a wooded glade. When it happens, it happens. Sometimes, not only does the Spirit of God cause the unexpected to happen, but He also brings together a whole variety of unrelated events for the single purpose of bringing glory to Himself. How very much I needed to understand that truth when surrounded by hundreds of refugees in the African jungle. Although I was not responsible for the horrendous needs of those surrounding me, I was responsible for responding to the leadings of the Holy Spirit whilst in those situations. It wasn't that God wanted me to do better, He only wanted me to accomplish His will, and there is a big difference.

Whilst travelling with my companion and friend Richard, we were greatly privileged to come across a group of Liberian refugees sheltering in the forest near to the Liberian border. Most of them were known to us as they were members of a church we had connections with. By God's grace, we were able to provide food for everyone who was there, and that night we were offered shelter in a neighbouring village.

The stories related to us by these Christians were horrific. They told us how the rebels had raced into their community, randomly firing automatic weapons from vehicles covered with human skulls, which forced the Christians to abandon their every possession and flee for their lives.

The following day was a Sunday, and collectively we decided to hold a worship service within a forest glade. I cannot recall the message I shared on that occasion, but I will never forget the tranquillity we all experienced as we worshiped God together within the cathedral of giant trees towering above us. We worshiped God in beautiful harmony with hushed tones, knowing that God was with us. Even though these people had lost every possession, the presence of God was beautiful.

Having completed the purpose of this visit to Sierra Leone, I returned to Freetown where I had a few days to wait for a return flight to the UK. During that short time, I was able to share with the people I was staying with, the concern I had for my friends still surviving in Liberia. I mentioned to them that I was looking for a way to reach Monrovia in order to help and encourage those I thought were still living there.

Thankfully, even as I received fragments of information, I at least knew some were alive, even though many were separated from family and friends. Because I still had resources with which I could assist them, I assumed it was God's will that I should make every effort to visit Monrovia, despite the desperate situation within the country.

Once again, God's unseen hand was helping me. Having shared my thoughts with the missionaries I was staying with, the same ones who had arranged my fortieth birthday party several years previously, I was amazed to discover that they were now the representatives for the Red Cross for all Christian missions in Sierra Leone. The Red Cross was the only non-military organisation using their own aircraft for relief flights into Monrovia. My friends, knowing that I wanted to help the Christian community in Monrovia, were only too willing to help with my quest. Accordingly, they booked a flight for me that would leave just two days later.

The same day on which my flight was booked, I came across a Liberian pastor I knew, Pastor John. Although we apparently met just by chance in Freetown, I know that our meeting was divinely orchestrated. Pastor John was also keen to return to Monrovia to attend to the welfare of any of his relatives or congregation members who might have survived the war.

Following a long conversation, we agreed to travel together if he could get a seat on the same plane I was booked on. Although I hadn't realised it, meeting Pastor John was yet another remarkable God moment. Without his help, I would never have found accommodation or protection from any of the many risks and dangers in the devastated remains of the city.

Amazingly, the next day, Pastor John was granted a seat on the same plane, and twenty-four hours later we flew together from Sierra Leone's Hastings Airstrip into Liberia's Spriggs Payne runway situated within the relative safety of the city limits. At the time, I had been informed that Monrovia was filled with unarmed rebels, who had hidden their guns from the Economic Community of West African States Monitoring Group (ECOMOG) forces now patrolling the city streets.

It was on one of those very hot and humid days that the skilful pilots of the Red Cross aircraft approached Monrovia's city airport. They had been careful to avoid possible areas of rebel gunfire by flying the little aircraft low over the swamps. We finally touched down smoothly on the damaged airstrip and came to a gentle stop beside the temporary immigration post, which was just a roofless burnt-out shell of a building.

There were no landing formalities, except for a quick check of our visa-less passports supervised by nervous and unsalaried immigration officers. As I looked around, I was amazed to see that the whole airfield was thickly covered with spent ammunition cases, including the runway on which we had just landed.

The signs of recent ferocious battles were clearly evident. There was not a building in sight that had not been looted, damaged, or destroyed either partially or in many cases completely. In the past, this area, known as the fish market, was the site of the local football field and in normal times would be a hive of activity. Today, however, only a handful of wretched souls slouched aimlessly around, scavenging for whatever could be found.

Pastor John's destroyed church was adjacent to the airfield, so he knew the area better than I did, and fortunately, he knew of a place where we might be able to find shelter for the night. Having managed to find a wrecked but drivable vehicle generously identified as a taxi, he negotiated with the driver the cost of conveying us to the supposedly "safe place" before nightfall.

Knowing a curfew would be imposed just before dusk by the united West Africa military forces (ECOMOG), after which all travel would supposedly be impossible, we were keen for the taxi driver to reach our destination. However, the driver could only nurse his battered vehicle in the general direction of our destination at a crawling pace due to the frequent enforced stops at all the army checkpoints. Each checkpoint was manned by a different section of the ECOMOG alliance from the various nations along the West Coast.

We had managed to trundle slowly along Tubman Boulevard in our hired bone-shaker when my companion suddenly ordered the taxi driver to take a sharp left turn just before reaching the well-known ELWA junction that boasted a dysfunctional set of traffic lights. We had turned onto a track I had never noticed before and following many complaints from the taxi driver concerning the state of the unkempt dirt road, we eventually arrived at a small encampment comprising about ten wooden huts. The huts had been constructed behind a low hill, screening them from sight of the highway, and were protected on all other sides by the adjacent swamps in which crocodiles freely swam and large snakes slithered.

As we struggled to climb out of the taxi, to my amazement two Canadian ladies appeared in the doorway of the nearest hut. They walked over together and greeted us. I must have been the first European they had seen for a while for they were obviously as surprised to see me as I was to see them. We had so many questions about each other, but what a wonderful moment it was for both them and myself to meet in that hellhole created by the rebels and to share fellowship together concerning the goodness of our God.

Pastor John knew them well, for he served with the same mission organisation as these brave Canadian ladies, although he didn't know they would be in Monrovia at this time. It transpired that these missionary ladies had chosen to remain within the war zone throughout the whole of the conflict to care for orphaned and abandoned children they had rescued from the streets of Monrovia. The missionaries and abandoned children were sheltering in this quiet and forgotten corner of the city.

Pastor John decided to return in the taxi back to the city centre where he planned to look for members of his congregation. Once again, I was experiencing the remarkable hand of God providing in a situation that was well beyond my control. Not only had

God led me to Pastor John, but now, through him, to these two incredible brave ladies.

The fact that they knew me previously, having attended the evening church service where I was once pastor, resulted in their having no hesitation in offering me a hut for a few nights. Wonderfully, they also provided me with a meal that evening and during the following days. Then wonder of wonders, or should I say "miraculously," they offered me the use of a battered, but working vehicle for the three days I planned to be in the city. At that time, there was hardly another private vehicle on the road as most of them had been destroyed, commandeered for use by the rebels, or shipped out of the county having been sold by the rebels.

Once more, God was doing more than I could ask, think, or even imagine; although Monrovia had been completely looted and destroyed, I lacked for nothing.

During the time I was there, I was very conscious of the fact that Monrovia was filled with combatants hiding among the remaining population. Everywhere I looked, I saw desperate, desolate, and hungry people controlled by a large contingent of West African troops. The troops themselves were very edgy whilst they sustained a temporary cessation to the hostilities.

For me, whilst surrounded by total destruction and finding myself in such a desperate situation, I was experiencing the grace of God providing everything I required for the next three days and all within just a couple of hours of arriving. It was a modern-day miracle. How can I ever doubt the God who watches over those He chooses!

On that first evening back in the nearly deserted city of Monrovia, after the Red Cross aircraft flight from Sierra Leone, I sat with the two brave Canadian missionaries outside their hut, listening to their stories and chatting until night fell. They seemed grateful to be able to offload onto someone who was willing to listen to them concerning all their recent experiences, including the rescuing of the abandoned and orphaned children. Although they had a ham radio, these ladies were desperate for news of the outside world, in much the same way that I wanted to be updated concerning the situation within the city.

Later, when we eventually retired for the night, the strangeness of that evening reached a climactic moment. In normal times, Monrovia city would be very active and extremely noisy with a multitude of amplifiers blaring out local music at full volume, an endless and insistent hooting of horns from all forms of motor vehicles, along with the general hubbub of a multitude of conversations.

However, on this night, after my hostesses had retired, I was sitting by myself outside my wooden hut in total silence. It was like the silence that sometimes occurs just before a clap of thunder explodes unexpectedly. At that moment, there was not a breath of wind, not a voice that could be heard, for everyone spoke in whispers. There was not a light to be seen, for no one wanted to reveal their position to rebels, robbers, army patrols, or even strangers. Not a single dog barked, for every dog had been slaughtered for food. Not a note of music was heard, for there was only anguish and pain within the hearts and minds of the people. Not a creature stirred, for the shock of complete and total destruction had silenced even nature itself.

Yet in a strange way, it was the silence that offered me the sense of security. I clearly remember listening within the protective bubble of silence, if such a thing is possible. A little later, as I lay on my bed surrounded by so many dangers, I had no sense of fear, for I knew I was in the "bubble of God's protection," being fully persuaded that I was in the place God wanted me. As others have written in similar situations, "The safest place in the world is the centre of God's will."

In the tropics, every day consists of around twelve hours of daylight and twelve hours of night. During the dry period, the sun normally rises between six and seven a.m. and within a very short time, both heat and humidity begin to rise rapidly.

Having risen early on this, my first morning back in the city of Monrovia, I was already making my way very slowly towards the city centre in the battered car I had been loaned. It was a slow journey, not only because of the state of the vehicle, but mainly because of the many checkpoints. The army personnel were never in a hurry, for there was very little for them to do as they hung around their checkpoints all day. With so few private cars on the road, army personnel tended to repeat every question and query every answer given. Eventually, I managed to reach Sinkor, the area where we used to live and where I had arranged to meet Pastor John.

Having met, we immediately began searching for anyone we might know. It did not take long to discover that most of the people who fled the country had not yet returned and among those who had remained, only a few had survived the murderous acts of the rebels. Eventually, having walked through the dusty and damaged area where I used to live with all my family, I came across a pastor friend and his wife. It was great joy and relief to discover this couple, who had survived the conflict. From the beginning of the rebellion, he and his wife had chosen to remain in the city in order to support those who had not, or could not, run for their lives. The fact that both he and his wife had survived the atrocities was miraculous. I knew them both very well and even more importantly, trusted them. The pastor had been very helpful in times past, and I felt comfortable leaving money with him for my friends if or when they returned to the city. A few months later I heard that these friends had received the money I had left with the pastor. What an honest man of God he was.

Sometime before midday, Pastor John and I agreed to separate from each other in order to walk through different areas where we used to live. I particularly wanted to be alone as I was struggling to come to terms with the utter destruction I was encountering. In my opinion, not even bombs dropped from aircraft could have caused more damage. Every building was razed or burnt to the ground. Every lamppost was riddled with bullet holes, indicating the ferocity of recent gun fights. Every electricity transformer had been drained of the oil it contained by gunfire so it could be sold by the rebels.

Eventually, I decided to walk along the dirt road that passed my old house. As I approached the property, I could not believe what my eyes were seeing. Miracle of miracles! Our old home was still standing. Not only was it still standing, it was completely intact! There was an undamaged vehicle in the car port, every window in the house was still intact, and not a bullet hole was to be seen anywhere in the building.

In the midst of all the surrounding devastation, the house stood out like a landmark; this had to be an act of God. I quickly discovered that a rebel leader had chosen the property for himself, and that no other rebel had dared challenge him about his living there or damage the property in any way whilst he was in it. Although I considered the possibility, I decided not to pay him a visit, but chose rather to continue on my way.

Before the war, the Sinkor area of Monrovia, where we used to live, was a very popular location for the planting and construction of new churches. As a result, church buildings had sprung up everywhere as there were no building regulations enforced or adhered to! It was into this newer area of development that I chose to search for people I might know, especially church leaders.

Having crossed the main but deserted highway, I passed Sofie's, our onetime favourite ice cream parlour, which was now destroyed, and

entered what had at one time been a more affluent area. It was clearly
evident that the ruined homes would have been single story buildings
surrounded by protective high walls complete with strong iron gates.
Most, if not all, would also have had night-time protection provided
by guards and watchmen.

Now, following the looting, along with the wilful and utter
destruction of every building, I was forced to pick my way very
carefully through mounds of rubble as I searched for signs of life. As I
carefully approached a small section of a standing wall, there was just
no way of knowing if any hidden danger was lurking behind it. The
chaos around me gave some indication of the horrors that had been
endured by its inhabitants.

Without warning, I suddenly reacted to everything I saw around me
and became overwhelmed at the sight of all the chaos and destruction.
I had seen enough; all I wanted was to immediately leave the area.
Having looked around and selected what I thought was a possible
route to escape the chaos, I carefully began picking a way back towards
the main highway when I unexpectedly froze—had I noticed what
was possibly a movement? Was there something out of place amongst
the rubble that once was a lovely house?

Having no idea of what possibly could be lurking, I made my way
forward as quietly and carefully as I could, step by step. I looked
and looked again at the spot where I thought the movement had
occurred; then again, I froze, unable to move. Slowly I realised that I
was looking at a living naked body which was hardly distinguishable
from the surrounding chaos. Whoever it was, was silently rocking on
their haunches.

As I stared at this distraught wretch of humanity hardly
distinguishable from the chaos around, I began to realise that it was
a young woman, possibly in her teens, who being in some form of

stupor, was completely naked and traumatised. To my shame, I did not know what to do. To approach her as a white man could add to her grief, so I chose to move away quietly, thinking there was nothing I could do.

What a failure I then felt. I tried to console myself by believing that other survivors would find her and hopefully help her. Yet deep within the recesses of my conscience, I knew that I had failed her, and not only her, but I had also failed God, and I had even failed myself. The very least I could have done was to have given her my shirt, even as Jesus suggested to those who would listen to Him. That incident has haunted me ever since. Despite the sensitivity, the embarrassment, the distress, and the complete absence of anything I could use to cover her, I deeply regret to my shame that I did nothing, and now I really do believe that I could have done better.

The following day, I decided to drive downtown into an area of Monrovia where our Christian bookshop was located. Throughout the whole journey, I experienced a strange sense of being just an observer to the destruction, rather than fully understanding that I was actually in the midst of all the chaos.

This led to my having a false sense of security in which I felt immune to terrors seen and unseen. The road I travelled on was still littered with empty shells, rubble, and burnt-out vehicles. Passing the Baptist church, I noticed that the whole of the upper structure had been blasted away by a rocket.

Just a few yards further along the same road is St. Peter's Lutheran Church. Within this building the worst single atrocity of the civil war occurred. On July 29, 1990, approximately 600 civilians were massacred as they sheltered and prayed to God in the supposed sanctuary of that building. The massacre was carried out by around thirty government soldiers loyal to President Samuel Doe. It was just a few weeks after the massacre, shortly after the corpses had been removed, when I entered the church. The outlines of the bodies where they had lain for days in the tropical heat still remained etched on the floor.

Moving on from the church, I continued to drive towards the city centre. I passed disaster after disaster until I finally reached the downtown area of the city. Around me were just a few people scavenging through piles of rubble, intent on rescuing any remaining item of their past livelihoods they could pluck from the ruins.

Without expectation, I suddenly came across yet another miracle of God. For at the junction of Ashmond Street and Front Street, our old Christian bookshop was still standing and it was fully intact. Not only was the building fully intact, but every book and Bible had remained on display, protected only by a plate glass window.

As I looked around, it was the only shop that had not been totally destroyed in this part of the city. As with our old residence in Sinkor, the property had sustained just one bullet hole, the bullet having penetrated the plate glass window without breaking it. This to me was surely another miraculous sign of God's power and grace. It had to be evidence of God's power and protection in the midst of the most heinous of circumstances.

As I stood there gazing in wonderment at this remarkable sight, the door of the shop burst open and a gentleman, still dressing himself, stumbled out and onto the road. He immediately began to interrogate me with an overload of garbled questions and statements.

Apparently, it turned out that he was a Ghanaian Christian army officer who had taken it upon himself to protect the Christian bookshop from looters. It was very obvious that he had managed to accomplish such a magnificent task.

Unfortunately, I was unable to answer all his questions or offer advice due to the brevity of my visit and the fact that I was no longer a member of that mission. Yet I was overwhelmed at the sovereign power of God, who had chosen to protect both our house and the bookshop with all their contents. Unknown to me at that time, God had plans for Liberia in which I would have some small involvement and during which several thousand Liberians would be blessed. As the apostle Paul wrote in 2 Timothy 1:12 NKJV, *"I know whom I have believed and am persuaded that He is able to keep what I have committed to Him until that Day."*

Regardless of all the challenges I encountered, all I have ever done is walk through the doors that God opened for me, knowing that He is able to keep both myself and those things I count as precious, safe for all eternity.

By this time, I was almost too late to make the return journey to my accommodation. The quiet streets were now almost completely deserted and the vehicle I was driving was the only one on the road. The checkpoints were manned by military personnel who, as night approached, were becoming more aggressive. This made the passing of the checkpoints more and more difficult, and it was now taking much longer to pass through the inspections than earlier in the day.

However, I was making slow progress towards my accommodation, but with three checkpoints still to pass, there was only twenty minutes of daylight remaining. I was stopped at the next barrier by troops from Guinea whose English was very limited. They were very slow to examine and interrogate me and by the time they let me through, I needed to turn on the single working headlight of the car.

This caused problems at the next checkpoint where the military personnel accused me of breaking the law for not having two headlights—such is life!

I was now beginning to think that it was too late to continue driving, as the curfew was now in force. I considered looking around for a sheltered area in which to spend a night in the car, but that would have been very dangerous. By this time, I had I arrived at the last checkpoint.

It was now dark (in the tropics night falls very quickly). An unseen army officer yelled at me to turn my solitary light off. Having complied, I sat very still in the car with my hands clearly on display, knowing that armed personnel had their guns trained on me. Eventually, two soldiers walked slowly over to me and began the interrogation I was expecting. As soon as they spoke, I recognised from their accents that they were Sierra Leonean.

Thankfully, I was able to respond to their questions with my limited Creole and was immediately accepted as their best friend. From that moment, they could not do more to help me on my way. Despite the time now being long past curfew, I arrived back at the camp where the two ladies had become somewhat anxious about their car, if not for me.

The following morning, I boarded the Red Cross plane for the return flight to Freetown and left Liberia with much to think and pray about. Once again, I had experienced God's amazing provision in making the flight possible, had seen first-hand the bravery of the two women called of God to rescue orphaned children, felt the pain of a young woman who had lost everything, and had come face-to-face with my inadequate abilities. But through it all, I had seen the miraculous protection and provision of God.

I left Liberia knowing there was much to accomplish, for I believed God was just beginning to open new opportunities for me to do better in assisting my friends in this devastated country.

Chapter 17

The Last Prayer for a Community

In Sierra Leone, there is just one narrow road leading out of the Freetown peninsula, which all travellers needed to use to reach the other towns and villages throughout Sierra Leone. At the village of Waterloo, which was the most congested point of the road, traffic was always chaotic. Waterloo was, and remains, a major termination hub for PodaPodas (local minibuses). The collector of fares on these vehicles (often referred to as the apprentice) was often seen clinging externally to the PodaPoda, shouting out its destination to waiting passengers as it sped and swayed dangerously.

Waterloo Village also boasts a roadside market where food and drink are available for thirsty and hungry travellers and where tie-dyed cloth and other hand-crafted goods are offered for sale as gifts for friends or for personal use.

Once clear of this congested area on the edge of the Western Area, the old and very straight, narrow one-lane British-built road ran west to east and was particularly dangerous in the early mornings and late evenings when the blinding low sun contributed to the many accidents involving speeding vehicles. For the weary and footsore refugees seeking refuge in Freetown's designated campsites, this, the last leg of their four-to-five-hundred-mile journey, was exhausting, seemingly endless, heart-breaking and dangerous.

It was because of the refugees that Richard (my African companion) and I were travelling to the small town of Koindu, situated in the far eastern part of the country. It was in and around this area that thousands of Liberian refugees were crossing from Liberia into Sierra Leone as they fled from the satanically inspired rebels. Richard, who originated from this area, knew it well, including local leaders and language, one of twenty-three spoken in the country. We knew from experience that it would take a couple of days to negotiate the approximately 280-mile journey, but we had no idea of the challenges that awaited us.

The road we travelled on passed through the town of Masiaka, named after a late president's wife, then bearing right towards the southeast we eventually reached Bo Town, where we made an overnight stop. Bo, known locally as Sweet Bo, is just what it says for the many travellers who have spent a night or two there. Sweet Bo Town always offered good and safe overnight accommodation in places like the Government Rest House. It even boasted a couple of decent restaurants, including the aptly named Black and White, where local meals could be enjoyed in comfort. Because Bo Town was located a few miles from the main highway on which the refugees were fleeing, we had a good night's rest in the tranquillity of quiet surroundings that helped to prepare us for the challenges we were soon to encounter.

It was still early morning when my companion and I left Bo to continue our journey towards the border town of Kailahun and then on to Koindu, where both Guinea and the Liberian border crossings were accessible. We managed to reach the town of Kenema in good time, but from there on, the hard-top road became just a dirt road that is partially levelled by a government bulldozer from time to time, and upon which vehicles speed, billowing up clouds of red dust that hangs in the humid air, until settling on everything and everybody on or around the tracks. These tracks became progressively more and more challenging as they wound their way up into the hills towards our intended destination. In some places, the road was nothing more than a dusty, bumpy, rock-strewn challenge as it ascended into mountainous regions.

During the dry season, this dirt track remains passable, but during the rainy season, with downpours of rain of up to 700 mm a month, it becomes every driver's nightmare. Some of the "mud holes" created by heavy lorries can be up to two metres deep. For those with smaller vehicles, negotiating these mud craters requires skill gained only though experience. Inexperienced travellers have been known to be stranded for days, waiting for help to have their vehicles extracted from the mud.

The route also includes having to negotiate several locally made primitive wooden bridges that need to be traversed with great care. Many of these were prone to collapse under the weight of overloaded lorries, resulting in the road being blocked for several days at a time. For the refugees trudging through this area, this track proved to be very challenging, energy sapping, and a great struggle for them as they headed for the refugee camps that were still two hundred miles away!

Whilst fleeing through Liberia, the refugees were unable to travel during daylight hours due to the possibility of being raped, tortured, or even killed if captured. Throughout the day, many were compelled to hide from the heartless rebels in the great Gola Forest. Then, without the aid of light, they had to find a way through the forest by following narrow hunters' tracks to reach and cross the international borders that were guarded and protected by defending troops.

Because of the irrational behaviour of the rebels, the refugees also had to make long diversions in order to skirt around rebel-held towns such as Voinjama and Kolahun. To add to their distress, the refugees discovered that having crossed the border into Sierra Leone, towns like Koindu, Buedu, and Kailahun appeared unwelcoming. The communities within those places had little or no food to offer the suffering travellers.

As we drove towards our intended destination, we passed columns of refugees. The only sound to be heard from them was the shuffling of their weary feet trailing through the dusty track. Walking in silence, the refugees occasionally lifted tired eyes from the endless road to glance at us in the hope of receiving a little food or water. It seemed that the rare sight of a white man in these regions was worth the glance, hoping that he might have something to offer.

As uncomfortable and useless as I felt passing these columns of humanity, our immediate and urgent objective was to reach the border between Sierra Leone and Liberia before nightfall, as spending a night on this road would be very dangerous.

Thankfully, we reached the village of Buedu during daylight hours and, unlike the refugees, were offered food, water, and a room for the night, for this was a village where my friend was well known.

Throughout this area, the international border between Liberia and Sierra Leone is mostly unmarked, and it seems to me that only the local inhabitants know where the border lies. The exception is the international crossing point, where a massive nine-foot double iron gate had been erected many years previously, marking the spot where the two countries meet. The gates had not been closed for many years, but with the imminent possibility of an invasion by the Liberian rebels, the Sierra Leone army had recently closed them.

On the Liberian side of the border is a tired old road sign that reads, "Welcome to Liberia," the only welcome being a long and dusty track disappearing into an endless plain of elephant grass.

In the past, I had travelled this road on several occasions when visiting pastors in the Kialahun area and addressing local pastors' conferences. Just before this trip, whilst back in the UK, I received news of terrible suffering endured by these pastors, along with other inhabitants of the villages, at the hands of the rebels.

It was reported that the pastors, in particular, had experienced a great and tragic event in which I inadvertently had some involvement. Before making the trip, we had shipped over two thousand Bibles in our containers that were gifted to the people of Liberia through the generosity of the UK Bible Society and the Trinitarian Bible Society. After the shipment had been cleared at the port of Monrovia, I insisted that some of the Bibles be sent to the pastors throughout the Kailahun area.

A few months later, despite the continuation of the atrocities being perpetrated throughout the area, I received news that the Bibles had been successfully delivered. I was thrilled at the news and very grateful to those who had helped transport them. Along with my friends, we gave thanks to the Lord for the successful delivery.

Tragically, our joy turned to sorrow, for very shortly after the Bibles had been delivered, I was informed that the pastors, along with other church members, had been shot dead for carrying the Bibles to Sunday service. It was said that one pastor was boiled alive, but I was never able to verify the truth of that, although I know it was a possibility. I was devastated by the news and felt some personal responsibility for the suffering of that Christian community.

Now, standing before the closed gates at the international border, just a few miles from where the pastors were killed, my heart and thoughts contemplated the possibility of visiting the surviving Christians in the surrounding villages.

Due to very high security throughout the area, we thought it would be an impossibility to reach this border crossing, yet here we were, standing at the gates. Nobody had stopped or challenged us. We did, however, come to the attention of the army major responsible under President Momoh for the defence of this location and discovered that he was of a Christian persuasion. Later, we learnt that his two sisters, who lived in London, gathered with other members of their local church to pray for him regularly.

The major, having accepted us into this restricted area as relief workers, gave permission for us to attempt negotiations with the terrifying rebels who would visit the crossing point from time to time.

The following day, as we stood at the border gates with the major, we saw the rebels approaching. They were heavily armed and those on foot were jumping in and out of the long elephant grass like jackrabbits. The major informed us they did this to lessen the possibility of being shot at. All the rebels wore masks of different shapes and sizes. Some had even incorporated the skulls of those they had murdered into their masks.

Amazingly, following erratic negotiations with these drug-crazed teenagers, they agreed to escort us to the village of Kailahun during the next few days in one of their vehicles, for a price.

Today, how I thank the Lord that those rebels never returned. Upon reflection, even though we had the best of intentions, I confess that it would have been the foolhardiest action I would ever undertake without a clear revelation of the will of God. Yet, as I was to discover, God had other purposes for us being at that border at that precise time, which we had not anticipated.

During the time spent waiting for an opportunity to cross the border, the major often spoke to us. The tension throughout the area was increasing daily, resulting in him asking if we would pray for members of the army who were the first line of defence against an anticipated rebel attack.

We agreed, and the next day, within sight of the border crossing gate, the major gathered together the army personnel who were available for us to pray with. Unfortunately, very few could attend, as the majority were on protection and defence duty.

In order to boost numbers for the time of prayer, the major turned to the adjacent secondary school and ordered all the senior pupils to leave their classes and attend the prayer gathering. At his command, the older children brought their chairs with them and assembled before us. Noticing what was happening, the other teachers sent their classes out to join us until the entire school body was assembled before us, swelling the gathering crowd.

I assumed that every adult, if not all the children who had gathered, knew what the rebels intended to do within days if not hours, but nobody was willing to talk about it.

Students without chairs were instructed to sit on the ground, and those with chairs sat behind them. This allowed the army personnel to stand at the back of the crowd with their guns ready for action. When all was ready, the major came forward and took a long time to introduce me. Finally, he turned to me and invited me to address the gathered crowd.

I was in no hurry to speak, for I knew this was a very difficult situation with an uncertain outcome. I took my time and for a few minutes just looked over the sizeable crowd now waiting in silence before me. In the prevailing silence, I pondered before God what I should say and how I should pray under these challenging circumstances. It seemed clear to me that the major knew what was going to happen within days if not hours, but what words of help or comfort could I offer these people at such a time as this?

Eventually, and with a very heavy heart, I turned and looked towards the heavens. In those moments, I reached out to the God who reigns in the heavens above and committed that moment into His hands, for I had faith to believe He could see all who were before me and would hear my prayer. There was only one thing I could say to those who had been ordered to gather before me in what proved to be the final message that the majority would hear.

I told them about Jesus and His love. I explained that Jesus Himself had faced death at the hands of cruel people and, in doing so, had provided a way for all of us to receive the gift of eternal life. Today, there is a way provided for all humanity to know God, receive forgiveness for every transgression, and live in the eternal presence of God.

Having shared these thoughts, I then read from the Scriptures and having prayed, committed them into the hands of God, whom the vast majority would meet before the week was out. The rebel invasion occurred just a few days later. Most, if not all, of those we had spoken to were ushered into eternity.

A thousand questions have crossed my mind since that day. Could I have said more, done more, given more? The answer has to be yes, but the real question must be, did I proclaim what God wanted me to say? Only God knows, and it has taken years of heart-searching to come to terms with difficult questions that arose in my thoughts concerning all I saw; the things I know, and the crazy things I attempted to do.

The only thing I can comprehend is that I know it was God who led me to be in the right place at the right time, for His own purposes. Could He have chosen someone else? I'm sure He could. But the conclusion of all my contemplation is that for reasons I do not understand, God chose me to pass on His message and to pray for those people facing a life-or-death crisis.

After several years, God's peace has settled my heart. How deep is that peace! How mighty is that peace! How miraculous is that peace! I cannot doubt that it is the very God of peace who chose me, sent me, and entrusted me with a message for a people at such a critical hour. For those assembled in that place at that time, the last thing they ever heard was a reading of the Scriptures.

On August 14, 2002, Fadiru B. Koroma of Freetown, Sierra Leone, wrote, "More than 100,000 people have been displaced along the border of Sierra Leone and Liberia since the beginning of this year, when fighting between the Liberians United for Reconciliation and Democracy (LURD) and troops of President Charles Taylor intensified. Now the situation along the border is becoming increasingly volatile, as troops loyal to Taylor make more frequent forays into Sierra Leonean territory in search—army spokesmen say—of LURD rebels and deserters from the Liberian army. As the fighting has worsened, it has become more difficult for aid agencies to reach refugees in the affected area". According to Monrovia's independent daily *The Inquirer*, which had placed a journalist behind rebel lines, there were more than 200,000 people living in deplorable conditions and hiding in the forests of Lofa County.

Almost twenty years after these events, I received an unexpected telephone call from a minister of a church in Taunton, a small town in Somerset, South West England. He was part of the local Christian leadership group who were to have lunch with a Liberian visitor. They called me to see if I wanted to join them, and I responded by saying that I had met hundreds of Liberians at different times and thought it better that the group meet the Liberian without me.

A few days later, the minister called again, informing me that they were outside a restaurant with the Liberian pastor, waiting for me to join them. I immediately felt obliged and embarrassed over the misunderstanding and set off to join them.

The group was still standing outside the restaurant when I arrived, and it was obvious who their Liberian guest was. Approaching him, I shook his hand with the Liberian handshake, which he refused to acknowledge. I then shook his hand for a second time, to which he responded. Feeling a little uneasy about this first encounter, I noticed a huge welt of a poorly healed scar across the back and a little to the side of his neck.

During the "help yourself" lunch, we were able to relax a little, and I discovered that he was an ex-member of the aforementioned LURD rebel group. Apparently, as with the vast majority of teenage rebels, he had been forced to join the group at gunpoint, but later escaped and subsequently converted to Christianity.

Having been captured by the rebels after deserting them, he was sentenced to death by beheading for desertion. The welt on the back of his neck was the result of a failed attempt to behead him. His life was saved through the assistance of my friends, the pastors of Kolahun. They cared for this ex-rebel who had at one time belonged to the group that murdered their friends.

He was seriously wounded, and they carried him in a local hammock, made of cloth tied at both ends to poles carried by two or more people, along secret forest trails to a hospital in Guinea where a Christian girl recognised him as a changed man. Today, this man cares for Liberian orphans, and his wife is a graduate of our computer school in Monrovia. I have to admit that I have found it difficult to accept him as a Christian, but even as Christ has forgiven me, so must I do unto others.

I share this, knowing there are unique times and occasions that offer just a once-in-a-lifetime opportunity to share God's Word and love. The devil whispers in my ear that I could have done better, but when I listen to those whispers, I lose not only my sleep but also my peace.

Yet, even when the devil whispers such things in my ear, the Holy Spirit speaks not to the ear but to my heart. He reminds me of scriptural promises, and I know that He who called me is faithful and He will do what He has said. I also know that where God leads, God always brings peace. Sometimes I need to wait in the presence of the Lord until His peace settles upon my soul, and only then can I say, "It is well with my soul."

Chapter 18
Knowing When "No" Is Right

As I reflect upon the amazing ways God has led, blessed, and protected us throughout our years of journeying, I am fully persuaded that God is faithful and prospers our ministries according to His purposes. Not that I regard prosperity necessarily as gaining personal wealth, although we lack no good thing. I understand prosperity in relation to God as His making us fruitful, totally secure, and always at peace. When we are in the place where God desires us to be, that is where He supplies our every need.

Our experience for many years has been as Moses wrote in Deuteronomy 8:14-17, *"Your God, who brought you out of the land of Egypt, out of the house of bondage, who led you through the great and terrible wilderness, with its fiery serpents and scorpions and thirsty ground where there was no water, who brought you water out of the flinty rock, who fed you in the wilderness with manna which your fathers did not know, that he might humble you and test you, to do you good in the end"* RSV.

The God who led us safely through various forms of danger is also the God who allowed us to rest in pleasant places—where we have always been refreshed in the quietness of His presence. This God is the God who, when we had nothing of this world's goods, provided everything we needed, even during the most challenging of times and situations. We have discovered that it is God who decides the times and occasions when He says, "yes" to our prayers and the times when He says "no."

Everything accomplished in our lives has been in accordance with His will; even the tough times. Our God is the God of the Bible, who is also the God and Father of the Lord Jesus Christ. In this God, I have the faith to go where He sends me and say what He gives me to say, even when I have been offered what first appears to be a better way.

Just a few months after accepting the opportunity to serve just nine people in a little country church, I was invited to visit the computer school in Monrovia that was now thriving. It had gained a good reputation and had become immensely popular.

Even though the situation in Liberia remained very unstable with marauding gangs of rebels still at large, plans were under way to enlarge the institution's training capacity. With the help of the West Africa Peace Keeping Force, a fragile ceasefire had been agreed upon, which offered a window of opportunity for me to make yet a further visit to Monrovia. Unfortunately, the international airports of both Sierra Leone and Liberia were closed due to the continuation of violent hostilities.

The only way left for me to enter Liberia was to fly in on a privately-owned Russian aircraft from Abidjan in the Ivory Coast, into Liberia's Monrovia city airport. Fortunately, I had good friends now living in the Ivory Coast who had been members of the church in Monrovia, and who were currently managing a Christian mission guest house. Having been informed of my plans to visit Monrovia, they extended an invitation for me to stay in their home for a few days whilst I made arrangements for a flight from Abidjan to Monrovia. The Russian outfit was using a three-engine aircraft, which looked more like a garden shed than a plane to me, and I was not happy at the thought of flying with them, but there was no other option.

The friends I stayed with attended the English-speaking International Church of Abidjan, where many Liberian Christian refugees were worshipping. Without informing me, they had recommended that I could fill the vacant pastorate of the church. Consequently, I arrived in Abidjan to discover that they had arranged for me to speak at both morning and evening services on the Sundays I was there. With some hesitation, I agreed to speak, but made it clear that I would not be speaking with the view of applying for the pastorate.

On the Sunday morning I arrived at the church, I was both amazed and very excited to discover several Tuareg families camping around the gates of the church's compound. These hardy and noble people had been forced to leave the Sahara Desert due to famine and were now reduced to begging for food whilst living in squalid conditions as destitute refugees. At the sight of their presence at the gates of the church, something stirred within me as I recalled my time in the Sahara Desert and the reasons I had gone there—to support the medical missionaries who were seeking to help these nomadic people.

The possibility of this encounter being another surprising "God-appointment" crossed my mind. Having met the Tuaregs unexpectedly, I felt the need to reconsider what God's will was pertaining to the invitation I had received to apply for the pastorate of the international church.

Altogether, that Sunday proved to be a remarkably interesting day as I met with the Ivorian congregation, the missionaries, the businesspeople, the Liberian refugees, and the inhabitants of the Tuareg encampment. These encounters left me with many issues to consider and pray over pertaining to what God's will was concerning the next step in my life.

Just two days later, I reluctantly and prayerfully took my seat in the three-engine propeller plane being flown by one or more of three

Russians seated on the raised and open flight deck for the flight to Monrovia. Following take-off, the pilots were clearly enjoying their own company as they laughed and talked to each other whilst sharing some form of liquid refreshment from a bottle.

For me, sitting in the fuselage, the aircraft definitely seemed to be rattling excessively as we flew low over the forest. Looking through a tiny window, I noticed one of the coverings of the plane's three engines was being held in place with a piece of twisted wire and realised that this was the reason that engine was rattling so much!

Travelling in such a strange aircraft gave me the feeling that it was "lumbering" through the air as though flying was hard work; but we eventually made it to Spriggs Payne landing strip in Monrovia.

As the aircraft descended, I once again noticed that the runway was still covered with spent bullet cases from recent gun battles. With a lot of bumping and excessive noise from the reverse thrust of the engines, the pilots managed to bring the aircraft to a standstill at the end of the very short runway.

Much relieved, I alighted (or was that escaped?) from the aircraft. After landing, the disembarking passengers were again directed into the "new" customs and immigration office that was in the same burnt-out shell of a building I was interviewed in the last time I had visited Monrovia.

This time, the immigration officers seemed to be intentionally intimidating us by making the arrival procedures quite difficult. We were instructed to enter into the gloomy darkened building and show our passports. Having just walked in from the very strong sunlight, I had great difficulty seeing anything or anybody inside the building. I eventually became aware of the shadowy figures of the officers and knew that they had the authority to grant us entry into the city or return us back to Abidjan on the plane that had just brought us.

A little name-dropping of the Minister of Education whom I knew, always helps at times like this and eventually my passport was stamped with a seven-day visitor's visa. The golden rule for travellers in these situations is never hurry, never raise your voice, never panic, and above all, keep smiling. Sooner or later, the experience will be over!

Having survived the ordeal of entering Liberia, I left the airstrip and thankfully discovered my friend Isaac waiting for me. Fortunately, his home, previously mine, was only a five-minute ride away in the dilapidated taxi he had hired. Grateful to be there, I was able to recuperate from yet another unforgettable and hopefully unrepeatable experience.

It was almost like being home as I entered our old house. Isaac is a faithful brother in the Lord, and it was a privilege to have helped him through the days of his being a refugee. With much energy, he was now developing a great vision for his nation through the development of a Christian-based computer school. The original five computers God had supplied were still in use and, since then, we had been able to send dozens more. He was still operating the computer training school in the adjacent YWCA, where many of the students lodged, but he was now looking for larger premises.

That evening, we chatted together over Isaac's experiences of fleeing from the Monrovian invasion, hiding in the Gola Forest from rebels, and surviving the refugee camp in the Ivory Coast. He shared how he had been separated from his wife and children, and how she and the children had hidden in a tiny room for three days and nights without food or water, when the rebels had occupied the same house.

The way God protected and provided for him and his family was amazing, especially during times of extreme, life-threatening situations. The money I had left for him with the pastor on my previous visit had been handed over to him, for which he was very grateful.

Later that night, having retired to my old bedroom, I slept on one of the ex-hospital beds we had shipped from the UK. Throughout that night, Isaac stood guard over me, patrolling the perimeter of the property's fence and ensuring that the armed and drunken rebels, sleeping only twenty metres away, did not awaken and approach us.

The following morning, as I surveyed the area around the property, I discovered that it was protected only by a broken wire-linked fence yet remained the only property in the area that had not been looted or destroyed.

Even more amazing was the miracle of God in the provision of clean drinking water for the entire surrounding impoverished local community. The very last task I had attended to before leaving Liberia was to have our garden well cleaned and refreshed. It had now become the only source of clean water for the whole area, as every other well had been contaminated with dead or dying bodies.

The rebels had murdered dozens of innocent people and cast their corpses into all the other wells to deliberately pollute the water. The rebel chief, who had taken over our mission house for his own use, had preserved this well for his own needs and it was now the only source of drinkable water for the entire community that had survived the massacre. This was undoubtably another of God's miracles in which He provided and protected our drinking water.

The grace and miracle of God extended even further; our house remained the only property throughout the whole district that was not destroyed, and now looked starkly out of place as it stood untouched although surrounded by the devastation. Inside the property, even the furniture was untouched. The house had been struck by just one bullet, which was still lodged in the wall of the lounge. This shot was fired in anger by the rebel leader when Isaac demanded that he should leave the house due to it being a God house.

Amazingly, the rebel left, and subsequently I was able to dig the spent bullet out of the wall and retain it as a keepsake, reminding me of God's power and protection. Having completed my business with Isaac, I returned to Abidjan the next day, unfortunately, in the same aircraft I had arrived in. With the salvaged bullet in my pocket and myriad thoughts chasing around in my head, I wondered what God would have me do next.

Arriving safely back in Abidjan where I was due to speak at the International Church of Abidjan again the coming Sunday, I agreed with some hesitation to be interviewed by the membership regarding the vacant pastorate. With the burgeoning congregation swollen by an influx of Liberian refugees, a Tuareg encampment squatting at the gates of the church, and many opportunities to serve God in West Africa, I had much to ponder.

Just a few days later, I prepared to return to the UK, where once again I was about to experience God doing the unexpected; for His ways and His thoughts are beyond anything I could imagine or expect.

Just two weeks after arriving home from Abidjan, I received a letter from the International Church of Abidjan inviting me to accept the pastorate. How I now needed to know the mind of Christ concerning this invitation. On the one hand, I was being offered everything that my missionary vision would love and desire. On the other hand, I had only recently accepted the responsibility of caring for just nine elderly saints in a little church hidden away in the Oxfordshire countryside.

Following a time of prayer, inner struggles, and family consultations, I came to my conclusion.

I needed to allow my faith in God to burst my bubble of Christian ambition, and accordingly, choose to stay where God had placed me. So, along with my family, we chose to remain with the little church.

Just a few months later, the Liberian rebellion spilled over into the Ivory Coast, resulting in much bloodletting and death. This would have caused my family and me to flee back to our own country for refuge.

Amazingly, just a few months after declining the pastorate in Abidjan, the little insignificant church hidden in the English countryside where God had so clearly led us, continued to experience only what God can do, the miracle of growth. People were experiencing being born again by the power of the Holy Spirit as they turned to Christ for salvation from sin and began to experience the blessing and power of God in their lives. Many visitors from other churches also began to attend the services (which I found difficult to handle). The outcome was that the financial giving at the church began to provide much blessing and provision for hundreds of God's people in West Africa. In many ways, I no longer needed to go to Africa to be a blessing in Africa.

Chapter 19
Fear – The Power of Witchcraft

The beautiful Liberian southwestern Atlantic coastline stretches for 260 miles, dotted here and there with a few coastal towns and remote fishing villages. Sierra Leone, to its northwest, is separated by the great Mano River as it flows through the mighty Gola Forest. Throughout the forest exist remote villages, accessible only by walking the forest trails, some of which are over a day's walk from the nearest navigable forest road for lorries.

With Guinea to the north and Ivory Coast on the east, Liberia's landmass is only a little larger than that of Scotland; yet it is homeland to an estimated seventeen ethnic people groups with a total population of around five million inhabitants. Although there are similar characteristics among all the people groups of Liberia, there remain language, tradition, and customs peculiar to each group.

The official Liberian National Census gives the questionable statistics that 86 per cent of the nation is supposedly Christian, with 12 per cent being Islamic. Even if that is true, it is common knowledge that many Liberians also maintain traditional tribal beliefs and practise pagan rituals. Many of the nation's inhabitants possess traditional charms and "medicine" for protection against seen and unseen forces of evil where polytheism is widely practised. In the midst of all of nature's wonder and beauty, the fear and control of witchcraft in all its forms, raises its ugly head.

These things, being contrary to the very heart of Christianity, are often the cause of the church being weak and vulnerable against the seen and unseen powers of darkness. A weak church has no power or authority against the various practises of witchcraft with all its vile forms of bloodletting, charms, potions, and reported acts of cannibalism.

Throughout the war, the power and fear of witchcraft were effectively used by rebel leaders of the various and divided warring factions, which led to the destruction of the nation's infrastructure and the slaughter of over 250,000 members of its population.

It is the power of fear associated with the secret bush societies and medicine men that compels many people to wear protective native amulets and causes nominal Christians to make various sacrifices for protection against unseen powers. It is fear that drives churchgoing people to engage with unscriptural rituals for protection and cleansing, including sleeping with the book of Psalms under the pillows for protection. The practice of placing a Bible in the foundations of a newly built house is thought to ensure that the house is "built upon the Word of God" whilst being protected from evil.

Stories of supernatural occurrences in Liberia, recorded by European travellers in their travel books, are remarkable, although personally, I do not believe all the stories I have read. Such reports include supernatural events supposedly performed by medicine men, or witch-doctors, including the metamorphic ability of human shape-changing.

I have been informed by trusted people about local rumours suggesting that powerful medicine men can control swarms of bees and other creatures, as weapons of war during times of conflict. There are also reports of various forms of bloodletting as part of initiation rites within the secret bush societies.

It is said that local medicine men can influence the action and confession of the misdemeanours of the indigenous people through the power of fear. Whether these stories and rumours are true is difficult to verify, but it is certainly correct to state that many people, from the homeless beggars on the city's streets to the rulers of nations, are ruled by the spirit of fear, which is a major satanic weapon. To my knowledge, every rebel leader, along with their enforced teenage troops, participated in various forms of satanic rituals ranging from accepting that there is such a thing as bulletproof medicine that protects them from being killed by opposing enemies with their guns, to wearing charms to protect them from spells cast against them, and taking potions for protection from opposing spiritual dark powers.

The driving power of these rituals is fear, fear that can only be demolished and made ineffective by the power of God's love, as the apostle John wrote, *"Such love has no fear, because perfect love expels all fear"* 1 John 4:18 NLT. John then clearly states in 1 John 4:16-17, *"We know how much God loves us, and we have put our trust in his love. God is love, and all who live in love live in God, and God lives in them. And as we live in God, our love grows more perfect. So we will not be afraid on the day of judgment, but we can face him with confidence because we live like Jesus here in this world"* NLT.

Somewhere and somehow the message that God's Love is greater than the devil's fear has been sabotaged, reducing Christianity to being just another religion, robbed of its dynamic power to change the vilest of sinners into children of the living God. Yet within the horrific circumstances of the Liberian and Sierra Leonean civil wars, there are testimonies of Christians who stood faithful and true to Jesus Christ, their Lord.

My friend Richard was invited to accompany pastors planning to visit remote villages in the Gola Forest. Towards the end of their trip,

I received a message inviting me to join them on the last evening of their mission.

It took a full day of driving to reach the village, and by the time we arrived, we were covered with red dust. Following a shower and an evening meal, we assembled in the "Palaver Hut," (the African village hall) just before nightfall, for a service.

Thunderclouds were gathering overhead, which shut out all traces of moonlight and left us totally dependent on flickering, locally made lamps for illumination. The darkness of that evening did nothing to dampen the enthusiasm of the villagers who assembled for the service. Within a very short time of being assembled, they were singing Christian songs and swaying to the rhythmic beating of the locally made musical instruments. Most, if not all, attending the meeting were filled with curiosity and expectation over the visit of the white man who had arrived, resulting in the village hut being full to capacity.

Following the normal long and over-emphasised introduction by the service host, which included all my unworthy virtues, the time came for me to share the Word of God. Fortunately, we only needed one translator on this occasion, as the villages all spoke the same language. As the message progressed, so did the heaviness of that stormy tropical night.

Suddenly and unexpectedly, a woman within the gathered assembly began barking like a dog. She was the local Zo (witch doctor), and her barking immediately caused tension in the meeting. Amazingly, my friends persuaded her to be quiet, and I was able to continue sharing the Christian message.

Following the preaching of the Word of God, an invitation was given for anyone wanting to receive further understanding of what had been said; or wanting prayer, to speak with a member of the visiting team. There was absolutely no response whatsoever to the invitation, which, within an African setting, was very, very unusual.

Being greatly disturbed by the events of that evening, I retired early and hardly slept due to fitful, restless thoughts churning around in my mind. That night I realised again just how powerful the forces of darkness are in the hands of those who have been captured to do its will.

At first light, I arose to find a simple breakfast ready for me on the table. No one seemed to be around, so I sat alone at the table, still struggling with the experience of the previous evening with morose thoughts. Then, in the midst of my negativity, one of the pastors suddenly burst into the breakfast room.

"Pastor Phil, Pastor Phil," he exclaimed enthusiastically. "Why are you looking so glum?" I just looked at him.

"Haven't you heard?" he said. I continued to blankly stare at him.

By this time, it had become obvious to him that I had not heard whatever the news was, and I was unaware of the reason for his excitement. He looked at me with his face beaming as he announced that the village witch-doctor had made a confession of faith in Jesus Christ the previous evening, after I had retired for the night.

At this moment, the whole village wanted to know more concerning faith in Jesus Christ for forgiveness from all evil, and eternal life with Jesus. I was quite shocked at this news and was immediately contrite over my lack of faith, but grateful once again that God had proven to be greater than all the forces of darkness.

I never had the opportunity to visit that village again, so I do not know how "Christianised" the community became. I do know that local pastors who spoke the language of the people of that village would have followed up on the events of that strange night. God's love, expressed and demonstrated by the pastors, proved to be greater than the powers of the witch-doctor that night.

Soon after breakfast, we said our goodbyes and left the village to begin our return journey to Monrovia. As the sun slowly climbed up and over the horizon, the road, made sodden from the storms of the night before, began to dry out and as it did so, I relaxed. As normal, the road was very rough as we passed through the mountainous areas. In some places, we had to stop in order to choose what we thought was the best way through the gullies and rocks, which we did with great care. Sometimes the way ahead seemed impossible, but by the grace of God, we always found a way, but not without the cost of time or damage.

In contrast to the mountainous area, which we had now cleared, the road across the plains and through the forest was relatively flat and incredibly dusty. The more we increased our speed, the greater became the clouds of red dust rising behind us. The dust hung in the air, lingering in the humid atmosphere.

When looking back, we could trace the road we had travelled on by that dust trail we had left.

When approaching villages or passing pedestrians, we always considered it necessary to slow down in order to lessen the amount of choking dust that would cover everyone and everything in thick layers.

In these remote areas, it was quite normal for pedestrians to signal for a lift, along with their goats and chickens, whenever we drew close to them. I have never discovered why, no matter which way the pedestrians were walking when we first saw them, they always wanted to go in whatever direction we were travelling.

As I travelled with my companion, sharing the events of the previous evening, we acknowledged that we had experienced the grace and power of God in a wonderful way and remained amazed at the way the evening had turned out to glorify God. We both knew that we had been in the presence of the Lord Jesus, during which the Spirit of God had triumphed over the powers of darkness.

As we recounted all we had seen and heard, the windscreen of the car suddenly exploded in front of us without warning, following a "thump" that sounded like the windscreen had been hit by a mango. Fragmented glass shattered everywhere, forcing us to come to a halt as quickly as possible.

Climbing out of the vehicle, there was nothing around us that we could see or find that had caused this incident. Apart from the "thump," there was no explanation for the incident except for clearly hearing something of great curiosity. All around us was the distinct sound of a loud blast from a secret society hunting horn. Four times we heard the unmistakable blast, but each time it was fainter and further away. It seemed that whatever was causing the sound of the hunting horn was travelling through the forested area on the wind. Was this a demonic retaliation for all that God had done during the past twenty-four hours? I know what I think, but I can only leave others to come to their own conclusion.

Many years later, having passed in and out of these West African countries throughout the wars, I asked myself where God is in these supposedly Christianised lands. Certainly not in the hearts of those who practised their murderous ways, or even in the hearts of those who turn to their ancestral fetishes for protection. Under the pressure of fear, stemming from the callous war imposed upon them, two basic reactions became visible. Some turned to Christ for protection, and others turned to their traditional charms and rituals.

Sometime later, following the encounter with the witch-doctor, I was invited to spend a day addressing the student body of a local Bible college in Monrovia. The students were keen and attentive as we discussed many issues relevant to their culture, using the Bible as our textbook. Inevitably, the subject of fetishes, particularly as used for protection against unseen evil forces, was raised. During frank and open discussion, most, if not all the students, informed me that they possessed traditional "charms" for protection against all forms of dangers that were purchased from so-called "medicine men" or sometimes "medicine women," some of whom led pseudo churches as prophets.

From personal experience, I know that these things have real spiritual powers that require faith in the Word of God and repentance before deliverance and freedom to minister the gospel are restored.

Following the reading and study of the Scriptures, the students themselves decided to burn the objects they had depended upon for protection. Having invited the Liberian principal of the college to join us, along with the leading missionary, without any form of condemnation, guilt, or secrecy, we committed our time together to God in prayer.

All the articles of so-called protection were gathered, wrapped together in strong brown paper, and tied with string. The fire, having been lit between the traditional three large stones, was then given time to reach maximum temperature. When all was ready, we gathered around the fire and placed the package upon the glowing fire logs.

All who had been invited to gather around that fire were of one mind, for we only had one purpose. For some, it was a very challenging and personal moment, being a costly event for most students as their traditional and pagan customs were being challenged, rejected, and exchanged for total faith and dependency upon the Lord Jesus, the teaching of Scripture, and the power of the Holy Spirit.

As the package was committed to the heated coals, there immediately and unmistakably appeared one word right across the package. In bold capital letters, the word *SPIRITS* appeared, which was seen by all who were present. There is no explanation for this unexpected event, but the impact upon the student body, the leaders, and myself is enduring.

Amazingly, I had discovered that extraordinary events such as these are not limited to remote areas of the world, where traditions and customs vary from those of the western world.

Whilst living and working with a church in and around the tranquil and typical British town of Henley-on-Thames, one morning there was a heavy hammering on the stout oak door of the Baptist church. This was unusual, for the coffee shop was open, and the door was unlocked because visitors were always welcome.

Because the hammering and battering on the door persisted with some force, I responded to the urgency of the moment in order to assist whoever was in some form of trouble. Upon opening the wide door, I was amazed to discover a group of about six male late teenagers. They were dressed in the style of the day and stood together in a tight bunch.

Without any introduction or explanation, the leader of the group held up a crucifix hanging from a chain around his neck, demanding that I immediately bless it. Their drawn and colourless features indicated that they had recently encountered some form of an unpleasant experience, so I invited them into the church where we could talk together in a quiet place.

They refused my invitation but continued with their demand that I bless the crucifix right there and then on the doorstep of the church. Eventually, the group began to understand that I wanted to know why they wanted me to bless the object they were waving under my nose.

With some difficulty, the leader explained that throughout the night, they had been engaged in a Ouija board session, during which the whole group had encountered a supernatural experience and communication. The resulting fear from this encounter had driven them to the doors of the church. Although I invited them once again to enter the church where we could offer a quiet room in which to talk about their experiences, they refused and walked away.

This was not the first time I had been requested to help teenagers who had experienced unexpected outcomes from Ouija sessions. Whilst in Liberia, we held a conversational Bible study for international businesspeople in our home every Tuesday evening. One couple who attended, were experiencing great difficulties in their Christian walk. Sometime in the past, our friend's wife had been in communication with the dark spirit world through a séance or Ouija board session. The resulting difficulty was that she would slip into a trance-like state every time the truth of Jesus was shared with her. Because of this phenomenon, we decided to set aside a time when we could pray together concerning this unusual situation.

On the agreed evening, we began by praying that God would keep her alert during our conversation and prevent her from slipping into a trance. What a joy it was to see her remain alert and participate throughout most of the evening. However, at an important juncture as we turned to God in prayer, she slipped into the trance.

I was so angry at the sinister force that had induced this situation that I commanded the unseen power to leave the woman immediately. In response to that command, the curtains at the window flew apart, and as they did, her husband leapt from his seat shouting, "It touched me! It touched me!"

Just how an unseen spirit force touched him I do not know, but what I do know is that on that night, God set that woman free, and she was able to confirm her faith in Jesus as Lord of her life.

Unfortunately, I have recognised the same dominating fear resulting from sessions of the Ouija board as I have seen in the lives of those who dabble and engage in pagan rites and rituals, even in so-called Christianised African places of worship.

Yet I know that the power of God through the Holy Spirit will break the power of fear in which the prisoner to fear is set free, for I have experienced it.

Chapter 20

Love – The Power of God

Many of my African friends have suffered at the hands of the rebels. Sitting down with those who were willing to share their stories with me has always been a challenging privilege. Not only did I receive first-hand reports concerning the atrocities these people of God suffered, but I was also informed of God's amazing intervention in their lives.

In addition to the uniqueness of these experiences, I was aware of the existence of God's higher authority ruling and overruling in what I can only describe as "the miracles of divine intervention and preservation." For me, such moments and occasions were clearly ordained of God. It is my sincere prayer that the lessons I learnt during those times will never be wasted. Even though at times I have been completely out of my depth, I have never been beyond the care and protection of God.

From among the pastors who knew their God, one story was repeated to me on several occasions. Having been captured by the rebels, sometimes the pastor who had been selected as the "object of entertainment" for the rebels' evening ritual, experienced God's amazing deliverance. Throughout the evening, as the rebels began to abuse the pastor, other prisoners were compelled to laugh, clap, and dance at gunpoint over the pseudo bravery of the tormenters.

One pastor informed me that having been questioned by the rebels, he was falsely accused of being from a wrong tribe. Subsequently, he was sentenced to death and bound to an execution stake. He shared with me how, having been bound to the stake, he was waiting to meet his Creator.

He went on to explain that at the very moment of execution, the peace of God unexpectedly came upon him and wrapped itself around him like a cloak. Immediately, he knew he was safe, either in the arms of Jesus, or he was about to experience a miracle. Along with others of my brave brothers, he was able to walk away from that execution post without explanation and began to comfort others in their distress.

Another pastor told me how he had been tied to a stake on the beach adjacent to the presidential mansion in Monrovia. As he stood waiting to be executed by a teenager, a little old lady walked up to the gunman who had been assigned to murder him and started to shake him.

She demanded, "Let that man go, let that man go, he's a God man." She then continued to harry the executioner until, turning to his commander, he requested permission to free the pastor.

Then, within those fear-filled circumstances and under the watchful eye of the drunken, drug-crazed, murderous commander, the pastor said, "I just walked away." This indeed was a remarkable God-given deliverance. Who was that old lady God used at such a moment—an angel or just a remarkably brave woman? Such men as these pastors have great faith in the God who rescued them out of their impossible situations.

My work colleague, Dewh, was fleeing with his wife and children from the falling bombs and streams of bullets being unleashed upon the city of Monrovia. As they ran for their lives, they had to pass through a rebel-held roadblock erected on the road leading towards the international airport. To their left were swamps, and to their right was the ocean; there was no way to bypass this checkpoint.

As the fleeing crowds passed through, Dewh was randomly detained by the rebels and subsequently thrown into a shallow pit, where he was held for execution as part of the rebels' entertainment later that evening.

His wife and children waited at the roadblock, pleading for his release, but along with others, who were also waiting and hoping for their family members and friends to be released, they were compelled to wait until evening. During the evening hours, they were forced to watch the rebels making sport of their loved ones.

As the evening wore on, the waiting crowd of onlookers was compelled to laugh, clap, and dance over the brutal antics of the rebels. Suddenly, those who had not been arrested were ordered to leave. As they did, they were ordered to sing, dance, and clap in admiration of the rebels' pseudo bravery. Anyone turning to look back for family or friends was threatened with execution.

By this time, Dewh had been taken out of the pit. He watched, as his family danced away down the road, clapping their hands as the rebels had ordered them. Dewh's family was convinced they would never see their husband or father again.

Later that evening, Dewh's time came to be "made sport of." He was brought forward into the arena where many of the other captives had been made to dance, were maimed, and even forced to eat parts of their own bodies to the jeers and laughter of the rebels.

As Dewh stood in the arena, one of the rebels suddenly shouted out, "I know this man; he works at the Christian bookshop. He's a

God man; let him go." Amazingly, or miraculously, the rebel leader immediately ordered his release.

Even though night had now fallen, Dewh was allowed to leave the roadblock and began to run after his family. He ran and ran the endless road that stretches for mile after mile in a straight line towards the international airport. He was determined to reach his family that same night.

Eventually, he caught up with them, and together, they gave thanks to God. What a reunion that family held for Dewh's deliverance. Dewh's wife is a woman who I know believes in miracles. Unfortunately, Dewh died a few years later from cancer, but I need to honour him as being a very brave man of God.

In a relatively safe place near the borders of Guinea and Ivory Coast, the Christians had set up a temporary camp where we had been able to offer meagre supplies. Late one afternoon, the lone figure of a woman was seen stumbling painfully into the camp. Following time for recovery, she was able to share her story of how her "Christian" husband had beaten her with a rod until she fled her home in Monrovia. She had undertaken the two hundred-mile walk through the jungle, seeking this place of safety that she had heard about, having lost everything she possessed, including her son.

Too drained of strength or energy to stand, the woman sat on the ground, unable to move. Unknown to her, my friend Richard, who was the leader of this camp, had already sent for a young boy to come and help her. Richard, turning to the exhausted mother, said, "My sister, your son is safe with us." A few moments later, we saw him walking towards us. With an outstretched arm, her son was slowly approaching.

Too exhausted to stand, the mother raised just one arm and as her son drew near with his outstretched arm, just their fingertips touched. For me, that moment was miraculous, for it seemed that the very power of life flowed from one to the other even as their fingertips touched. Through all the horrors of living hell that this saint of God had experienced, she was now receiving the healing comfort of a heavenly touch from her son as the saints of God attended to her needs.

Nathaniel Bimba, the pastor of a church in the town of Zorzor in northeast Liberia, was captured by the forces of Charles Taylor and taken into one of Taylor's jungle strongholds where the rebel leader was sheltering to avoid other rebel factions. His jungle camp was surrounded by a double wooden stockade, decorated with human skulls fixed on top of protective poles to ward off dark spirits and opposing rebels.

Whilst imprisoned in that camp, Nathaniel, along with his friend, were bound with wire in the torturous method known as the "chicken strap," a method of restraint in which both arms of the prisoner are so tightly bound behind their backs that it causes the shoulder blades to lift.

During the day, he was kept in a shallow trench, covered by sheets of corrugated iron, and given very little water to drink even as the tropical sun beat down upon them. In such circumstances, life became unbearable as he lay there day after day under the midday sun.

In the evening, Taylor would have Nathaniel brought out and, amazingly, questioned concerning his faith in Christ. Taylor also inquired of Nathaniel about the teachings of Scripture. Incredibly, even Taylor, at the height of his barbaric and murderous ways, professed some allegiance to Christianity. One day, without explanation, Taylor unexpectedly ordered Nathaniel's release.

A few weeks following Nathaniel's release, my friend Richard and I were travelling on a very remote and lonely jungle road when Richard suddenly commanded me to stop the vehicle I was driving immediately. Having complied with his instruction, I looked up and noticed an old Toyota coming slowly towards us. Unsure why Richard was so forceful in his instruction, I was uncertain whether to run, hide, or wait to see what would happen.

Having chosen the latter, I watched as Richard, who had by this time got out of our vehicle, was already some way ahead of me and was now waving the Toyota down. The driver of the oncoming vehicle, having seen Richard waving him down, stopped at the side of the dirt road. The driver's door opened very slowly, maybe even painfully. The driver alighted, and there, standing in the middle of the road, was that great man of God, Nathaniel, Richard's great friend, and the pastor who had been held captive by Taylor.

On that deserted road, I saw for only the second time in my life, that peculiar deep and meaningful African greeting, whether intentional or not I will never know. There was none of the normal African embracing, hugging, jumping, shouting, or jubilation at the reunion. I watched spellbound as these great friends drew closer together and slowly raised their right hands. Then, with arms outstretched, they allowed just their fingertips to touch. It was as though they were both reaching out to each other and in doing so were spanning periods of great pain and sorrow in which each was helping the other to come to terms with what they had experienced.

What a privilege it was for me when I was able to encourage Nathaniel with the promises of God. Within just a few months, he and his wife moved to East Africa and later to North America. Heaven will be the richer when these saints of God walk towards the throne of Christ with right arms outstretched towards the welcoming arms of Jesus.

Some years later, Taylor supposedly made a public confession of conversion to Christianity before thousands of Liberians during a massive Christian crusade held by an American TV evangelist As my friend Dewh said in response to Taylor's public profession of faith, "He never apologised to me for killing hundreds of my people."

Taylor's rebellion had also spilled over into Sierra Leone, mostly because of the bounty to be harvested from the diamond fields. Many of Sierra Leone's youth joined the rebellion either by choice or at gunpoint, resulting in thousands of civilians suffering through the brutal, uncontrollable, and undisciplined youthful uprising.

Throughout the fourteen years of the civil war, an estimated 300,000 civilians lost their lives. These teenage gunmen were very much controlled by the unseen forces of darkness and accordingly wore amulets and charms for protection. All were compelled to participate in various forms of satanic rituals. As a result, thousands of innocent people suffered. Today, many of the victims continue to suffer in silence due to what they experienced, saw, or felt. Their numbers and their pain are incalculable, but for victims and rebels alike, the power of transformation and reconciliation is found in the love of God.

Chapter 21
A God That Can Be Trusted

As already mentioned, my understanding of a miracle is an extraordinary event that cannot be explained by any human activity or force of nature, and is therefore attributed to being a divine intervention. Over the years, the occasion of divine interventions, during which God's provision, protection, and guidance, are so numerous that I can only conclude that there is a God in heaven whose hand of grace and mercy has been upon my family and myself. Some of our challenging situations have been so tenuous that, humanly thinking, it was foolishness even to confront them. Yet by faith in God and His Word, we always overcame whatever obstacles the forces of evil threw at us. As believers in God, we are not exempt from the challenges of life, but we are certainly not destroyed by them.

Over the years, I have had opportunities to attend and even participate in widely publicised African miracle crusades, during which international evangelists made bold claims concerning mass conversions, healings, and miracles. Having seen first-hand the immediate and long-term outcome of these events, I prefer to keep my observations and thoughts concerning modern-day miracles to myself.

In contrast, I have had the privilege of standing alongside my African brothers and sisters during times of great danger and need. This has permitted me to be party to their thoughts, feelings, and opinions concerning miracles. Our conclusion is that we do believe in the God of miracles because He protects provides, delivers, feeds, heals, and at times, wraps His cloak of divine peace around us, especially during times of crisis and close danger. We have complete faith in His love, power, and compassion. What God wills, will be done on earth. Why do we believe in miracles? Simply because we have experienced them, but not always in expected ways.

I was present at one of our Christian computer training graduation ceremonies. As is normal at these events, we had a very full programme, which included a past graduate soloist, who sang her story in a song. Her sung story recounted how she had fled Monrovia amid the bombs and bullets raining down on her as she carried her newborn child in her arms.

Reaching the coast, she managed to obtain a seat for herself and her baby in a convoy of several locally made fishermen's dugout canoes. The fishermen immediately paddled the canoes away from the danger zone towards Freetown. Sadly, when they were well out at sea, the little flotilla was hit by a tropical storm. With the storm raging, the canoe, in which the mother and child were sailing, was violently tossed around in the waves, so much so that her baby was swept from her arms. Whilst still clutching the sides of the canoe, she was forced to watch her baby sink beneath the waves.

As she sang her mournful song, it deeply moved us to tears, yet her love and faith in God shone through her pain. Oh, the agony that she and so many refugees endured throughout the trauma that was unleashed for years upon the citizens of those nations.

As we listened to her story, the entire class of graduates and their guests were moved with compassion and sympathy for the soloist, whose story reflected the pain of their entire nation.

As guest speaker at this graduation ceremony, what comfort from the Scriptures could I offer those who had for years walked through the valley of death? I could only empathise by reminding the gathering that there are times when, with God, we may not fear the evil, yet nevertheless we still have to endure our cross, even as Jesus endured His.

This woman had not rejected God because of the loss of all she loved and cherished, despite her personal suffering or even the bereavement over her lost child. Amazingly, her faith was so strong that she fully believed her child was eternally safe in the arms of her heavenly Father. As she continued to sing her story, she informed us of how God had provided for her and the Christian friends who supported her following her dangerous journey across the sea and the loss of her child. Within all these extremely challenging circumstances, her faith in God outweighed the craziness of the rebels and had remained firm during these extremely dangerous and tragic circumstances.

On another occasion, when travelling away from the international border, even as the rebels were breaking through into Sierra Leone from Liberia, we came across an abandoned aircraft hangar on a disused airfield. Within the hangar was a large group of Liberian people who were sheltering, having fled from the rebels. As I walked through the hangar, I was feeling very self-conscious, as I was the only foreigner there and every eye was watching me.

Eventually, in our random walk through the hangar, we came to a section that was partly shielded by a blue tarpaulin hanging from the struts of the roof. Peering behind the tarpaulin, we discovered a pastor, along with his wife, whom we knew. They had with them a large group of children, who having lost their parents, were now being cared for by this pastor and his wife. We encouraged them all with a few gifts to help them on their way and regretted that we could not do more for them.

On our departure, the pastor had a quiet word in our ears and informed us that his wife, a diabetic, had used up all her medicine. It was now impossible for her as a refugee to obtain more of the medication she depended on. He showed us their last empty package of the medication she required and, following prayer, we continued on our journey.

The next major town we came to was Kenema, where amazingly, we were able to rent a metal container in which we could spend the night. Inside the container were two beds, two chairs, and a bowl of water that had been placed on a stand. Having secured this safe place in which to spend the coming night, we drove around the town looking for a chemist. Almost every shop in Kenema had been closed and shuttered due to the floods of refugees roaming the streets; but we did come across a chemist's shop that was still open. Entering the shop, we noticed that almost every shelf was bare, yet the chemist was continuing to do the best he could to assist those who entered his shop with ailments.

As we looked around at the bare shelves, we spotted up on a top shelf all by itself, the exact medicine the pastor's wife required. We were both excited and amazed at discovering this correct medication. Unfortunately, it was the last and only pack containing the medication she needed. Having purchased the medicine, we immediately drove back to the disused airfield and handed it to a very relieved pastor and his wife.

Although we left them sufficient support for their immediate needs, I do not know how God continued to supply the needs of the pastor and his wife, along with all the children in their care. But I do believe in a God who has promised to take them, and us, through dark times.

We then drove back to our container, only to endure one of the most challenging nights of my life, as I attempted to sleep in that hot, stuffy, breathless temporary container. With the doors closed on that tropical night, it was so pitch black I could almost feel the darkness. Yet because of our faith in God, we were able to endure that night, and came through all those events by His grace and love.

Time and again I have experienced God providing unexpected accommodation, transportation, protection, and companionship amid various dangers, including nights in the jungle and days in devastated cities. Maybe above all, I have discovered that God's timing is impeccable, for He has often led me to be in the right place at the right time to meet the right people, but sadly I have not always realised God's divine purpose for those meetings.

If God desires His message of love and salvation to be proclaimed and demonstrated, not only to the wealthy, the educated, and the advantaged of this world, but also to the poorest of the poor, the captive, the oppressed, and those who live in remote places, who am I to say "no" if God has chosen me to send as His messenger, even if it is into difficult and dangerous places.

Jesus Himself indicated in Mark 10:27 that, *"Humanly speaking, it is impossible. But not with God. Everything is possible with God"* NLT. When our decision to follow God is underpinned by our complete trust in Him, we begin to realise that we can accomplish every task He asks and expects of us. It is also the moment when every step of obedience we take in response to His revealed will, becomes an act of faith with *A God That Can Be Trusted.*

Inspired To Write A Book?

Contact
Maurice Wylie Media
Your Inspirational Christian Publisher

Based in Northern Ireland and distributing around the world.

www.MauriceWylieMedia.com